READINGS ON

MOBY-DICK

ᴏMSON
GALE

Press is an imprint of The Gale Group, Inc.,

re trademarks used herein under license.

/www.gale.com

CATALOGING-IN-PUBLICATION DATA

Obstfeld and Loretta Obstfeld, book editors.
s literary companion to American literature)
es and index.
k. paper) —
aper)
. Moby-Dick. 2. Psychological fiction, American—
s, American—History and criticism. 4. Whaling in
, I. Obstfeld, Raymond. II. Obstfeld, Loretta.

2002192517

e United States of America

READINGS ON

MOBY-DICK

Other titles in the Greenhaven Press Literary Companion Series:

American Authors

Maya Angelou
Stephen Crane
Emily Dickinson
William Faulkner
F. Scott Fitzgerald
Robert Frost
Nathaniel Hawthorne
Ernest Hemingway
Arthur Miller
Flannery O'Connor
Eugene O'Neill
Edgar Allan Poe
John Steinbeck
Mark Twain
Walt Whitman
Thornton Wilder

American Literature

The Adventures of Huckleberry
    Finn
The Adventures of Tom Sawyer
All My Sons
Billy Budd
Black Boy
The Call of the Wild
The Catcher in the Rye
The Crucible
Death of a Salesman
Ethan Frome
Fahrenheit 451
A Farewell to Arms
The Glass Menagerie
The Grapes of Wrath
The Great Gatsby
My Antonia
Native Son
Of Mice and Men
The Old Man and the Sea
One Flew Over the Cuckoo's
    Nest
Our Town
The Pearl
A Raisin in the Sun
The Red Pony
The Scarlet Letter
A Separate Peace
The Short Stories of Edgar Allan
    Poe
The Sun Also Rises
To Kill a Mockingbird
Twelve Angry Men
West Side Story

T

© 2003 by Greenhaven Press. Greenh
a division of Thomson Learning, Inc.

Greenhaven® and Thomson Learning™

For more information, contact
Greenhaven Press
27500 Drake Rd.
Farmington Hills, MI 48331-3535
Or you can visit our Internet site at h

Cover credit: © Bettmann/CORBIS

LIBRARY OF CONGR

Readings on Moby-Dick / Raymc
    p. cm. — (The Greenhaven P
Includes bibliographical refere
ISBN 0-7377-0442-X (lib. bdg. :
ISBN 0-7377-0441-1 (pbk. : alk.
    1. Melville, Herman, 1819–18
History and criticism. 3. Sea sto
literature. 5. Whales in literatu
III. Series.
PS2384.M62 R43 2003
813'.3—dc21

Printed in

66I have written a wicked book, and feel spotless as the lamb.99

—Herman Melville, in a letter to Nathaniel Hawthorne, November 1851.

CONTENTS

Chapter 1: The Art of *Moby-Dick*

Chapter 2: Symbols and Themes in *Moby-Dick*

Chapter 3: The Use of Religion in *Moby-Dick*

FOREWORD

> *"'Tis the good reader that*
> *makes the good book."*
>
> Ralph Waldo Emerson

The story's bare facts are simple: The captain, an old and scarred seafarer, walks with a peg leg made of whale ivory. He relentlessly drives his crew to hunt the world's oceans for the great white whale that crippled him. After a long search, the ship encounters the whale and a fierce battle ensues. Finally the captain drives his harpoon into the whale, but the harpoon line catches the captain about the neck and drags him to his death.

A simple story, a straightforward plot—yet, since the 1851 publication of Herman Melville's *Moby-Dick*, readers and critics have found many meanings in the struggle between Captain Ahab and the whale. To some, the novel is a cautionary tale that depicts how Ahab's obsession with revenge leads to his insanity and death. Others believe that the whale represents the unknowable secrets of the universe and that Ahab is a tragic hero who dares to challenge fate by attempting to discover this knowledge. Perhaps Melville intended Ahab as a criticism of Americans' tendency to become involved in well-intentioned but irrational causes. Or did Melville model Ahab after himself, letting his fictional character express his anger at what he perceived as a cruel and distant god?

Although literary critics disagree over the meaning of *Moby-Dick*, readers do not need to choose one particular interpretation in order to gain an understanding of Melville's novel. Instead, by examining various analyses, they can gain numerous insights into the issues that lie under the surface of the basic plot. Studying the writings of literary critics can also aid readers in making their own assessments of *Moby-Dick* and other literary works and in developing analytical thinking skills.

The Greenhaven Literary Companion Series was created with these goals in mind. Designed for young adults, this unique anthology series provides an engaging and comprehensive introduction to literary analysis and criticism. The essays included in the Literary Companion Series are chosen for their accessibility to a young adult audience and are expertly edited in consideration of both the reading and comprehension levels of this audience. In addition, each essay is introduced by a concise summation that presents the contributing writer's main themes and insights. Every anthology in the Literary Companion Series contains a varied selection of critical essays that cover a wide time span and express diverse views. Wherever possible, primary sources are represented through excerpts from authors' notebooks, letters, and journals and through contemporary criticism.

Each title in the Literary Companion Series pays careful consideration to the historical context of the particular author or literary work. In-depth biographies and detailed chronologies reveal important aspects of authors' lives and emphasize the historical events and social milieu that influenced their writings. To facilitate further research, every anthology includes primary and secondary source bibliographies of articles and/or books selected for their suitability for young adults. These engaging features make the Greenhaven Literary Companion Series ideal for introducing students to literary analysis in the classroom or as a library resource for young adults researching the world's great authors and literature.

Exceptional in its focus on young adults, the Greenhaven Literary Companion Series strives to present literary criticism in a compelling and accessible format. Every title in the series is intended to spark readers' interest in leading American and world authors, to help them broaden their understanding of literature, and to encourage them to formulate their own analyses of the literary works that they read. It is the editors' hope that young adult readers will find these anthologies to be true companions in their study of literature.

INTRODUCTION

Unlike many other American novels deemed classic, such as *Huckleberry Finn* or *Catcher in the Rye*, *Moby-Dick* tends to scare first-time readers. It is a heavy book, with lots of pages, and, for all the whale-crushing-sailors action promised by some cover art, not a whole lot really happens. Worse, a lot of critics call it "a work of genius," which usually turns first-time readers off. However, for the person who chooses to persevere, *Moby-Dick* will be one of the most pleasurable and moving reading experiences of a lifetime.

When Herman Melville wrote *Moby-Dick*, he challenged the norm regarding what everyone at that time considered to be the proper way to write a novel. Instead, he made up words, included chapters set up like plays, and attacked political and social sacred cows such as racism, capitalism, imperialism, and religion. He included meditations on science, morality, hypocrisy, mythology, and anthropology. And he wrapped all that around the exciting plot of one man's obsessive hunt for the mysterious white whale that had snapped off his leg.

The articles presented in this book will explore various aspects of the novel, from the techniques and craft that Melville used, to the themes of self-discovery and social commentary that helped elevate the novel beyond just another sea adventure. It also explores the individual characters that, though they share the same voyage on the *Pequod*, are each on different types of personal quests.

But *Moby-Dick* is not just about its lofty ideas and troubled crew, it is also exceptionally funny. Inspired by Shakespeare's deft use of comedy even in his darkest tragedies, Melville found many passages to display his broad sense of humor. The development of prim Ishmael's relationship with the African "savage" Queequeg offers several farcical scenes that play out like the best television sitcom. Fleece's sermon to the sharks, like the wittiest *Saturday Night Live* skit, is at once hysterically satiric and insightful about human nature.

Finally, what makes *Moby-Dick* such a monumental work is that it is considered a truly American work of "literature," employing the delicate combination of complex characterization, weighty themes, and artistic writing technique that most critics of the time believed could only be found in writers from other, more sophisticated countries. The consensus before *Moby-Dick* was that Americans had no literary tradition, contenting themselves to merely imitate European literature. In 1840, in his widely popular and influential meditation on America, *Democracy in America*, Alexis de Tocqueville describes what he imagined American literature would be like:

> By and large the literature of democracy will never exhibit the order, regularity, skill, and art characteristic of aristocratic literature; formal qualities will be neglected or actually despised. The style will often be strange, incorrect, overburdened, and loose, and almost always strong and bold. Writers will be more anxious to work quickly than to perfect details. Short works will be commoner than long books, wit than erudition, imagination than depth. There will be rude and untutored vigor of thought with great variety and singular fecundity. Authors will strive to astonish more than to please, and to stir passions rather than charm tastes.

Eleven years after this was written *Moby-Dick* came along to embody some of what Alexis de Tocqueville predicted. Indeed, Melville had written a great, powerful book that was at once artful and sloppy, farcical and insightful, exciting and ponderous. It seemed fuel-injected by its own lust for life, romantic naïveté, and youthful passion to know everything. In other words, it defined the American spirit and thus became our first, and some say greatest, example of American literature. To read it is to lose oneself in the dangerous voyage of its crew, but also to find one's place in American tradition.

HERMAN MELVILLE: A BIOGRAPHY

Herman Melville began his writing career as the mildly popular author of adventure stories that fictionalized his own experiences as a sailor. Had he continued writing those simple melodramatic tales he probably would have been much more financially successful in his own lifetime—but completely forgotten in ours. Instead, like some literary Dr. Frankenstein, he decided to create an entirely new form of novel by stitching together body parts from the traditional sea adventure potboiler, Shakespearean tragedy, epic poem, and complex ideas from science, religion, philosophy, and politics. The result was *Moby-Dick*, a work of art that has continued to amaze and delight readers for over 150 years, earning it a prominent place on the must-read shelf of American literature. But chasing literary fame and fortune proved more dangerous and destructive to Melville than pursuing whales.

A HERITAGE OF HEROES

Herman Melville was born on August 1, 1819, in New York City, the third of eight children. His father, Allan Melvill, made a comfortable living as a wholesale merchant and importer. His mother, Maria Gansevoort Melvill, was the daughter of General Peter Gansevoort, a well-respected and wealthy Revolutionary War hero. Allan Melvill's ancestors were not as prosperous as his wife's, but they also had a distinguished history. His father had dressed as an Indian and participated in the infamous Boston Tea Party, subsequently serving honorably in the American army. As a boy, Melville had often seen the bottle his grandfather kept on the mantle, which contained bits of tea he had shaken from his clothes following the tea party. From both sides of the family, he inherited a strong sense of political awareness and pride in American history.

Though his father's business success was relatively modest, the household Melville was raised in contained a cook, a nurse, and maids. Much more important, it also contained furniture, art, books, and knick-knacks from various parts of the world, especially Europe. His father had been a great traveler, having covered, by his own account, "by land 24,425 miles, by water 48,460 miles." He had been at sea 643 days and once lived in Paris for two years. All this seemed to fire young Herman's imagination and whet his own appetite for travel.

A LEGACY OF FAILURE

The failure of Allan Melvill's import business in 1830, followed by his death in 1832, left eleven-year-old Herman with an even more lasting legacy: poverty. The family, which had moved to Albany after the business's collapse, was plunged into deeper financial debt. The embarrassment may have prompted Maria Melvill to add the "e" to her last name. Everyone had to pitch in to make ends meet. Gansevoort, the oldest son, took over his father's felt and fur business. Fifteen-year-old Herman took a job as a bank clerk at the New York State Bank, where his Uncle Peter was a trustee. After a year he quit to help his uncle, Thomas Melvill, on a farm in Pittsfield, Massachusetts, the town where he would later write *Moby-Dick*. Within a few months, Melville returned to Albany to help Gansevoort in the family business. The necessity to earn money had a sobering effect on the young teenager. As Melville biographer Lewis Mumford states,

> All Herman's ambitions, to go to college, to become an orator like Patrick Henry, to become a great traveler, like Uncle John or Papa, or to become a great general, like Grandfather Peter, to live in Paris, like Uncle Thomas, to make the name Melville somehow glorious—all these dreams were like great bonfires suddenly drenched by cold rain.

Despite these financial setbacks, the Melvilles scrounged enough money to send young Herman to Albany Classical School in 1835. Shortly afterward, he began teaching school in Pittsfield, but after three months abandoned that, too. Depressed and without a clear direction in his life, he returned home to Lansingburgh (now Troy), a small river village outside Albany where his mother had moved when Gansevoort went bankrupt. Melville took one more stab at the traditional career path by studying surveying at Lansingburgh

Academy with the hopes he would land a job on the Erie Canal project. During this time, he published his first known literary compositions under the pseudonym L.A.V. Titled "Fragments from a Writing Desk," they were published in the *Democratic Press and Lansingburgh Advertiser* in May of 1839. When the surveying job did not come about, Melville was again depressed, and again without hope for a secure future.

HIS FIRST TASTE OF THE SEA

In the first paragraph of *Moby-Dick*, Ishmael reveals his own remedy for depression: "Whenever I find myself growing grim about the mouth; whenever it is a damp drizzly November in my soul; whenever I find myself involuntarily pausing before coffin warehouses, and bringing up the rear of every funeral that I meet . . . then, I account it high time to get to sea as soon as I can." And so, in June of 1839 twenty-year-old Melville left behind the grim poverty of family life and shipped out as a cabin boy on the *St. Lawrence*, a merchant ship sailing from New York to Liverpool, England.

The voyage did not transform him into a sea-worshipper. In fact, in the four-month voyage he came to see the sailor's life as particularly brutal. As a cabin boy, he would have had to do the most menial of tasks, including cleaning pigpens and chicken coops on deck, unpleasant duties he would detail later in his novel *Redburn*. He returned home to begin the futile and humiliating search for work. His family was still in desperate financial straits, relying on charity from relatives to survive. Melville managed to find another teaching job, but the school closed due to lack of money and he was never paid.

In June of 1840, with no promising prospects at home, Melville and his close friend Eli Fly traveled west to Illinois, where his Uncle Thomas had moved. But Uncle Thomas was in no position to offer them jobs and the two friends boarded a steamer on the Mississippi River. Although no work came out of the trip, the steamer excursion provided details for the setting in his future novel, *The Confidence Man*.

By fall of 1840, Melville and Eli arrived in New York City in search of work. Eli quickly found a job, but Melville did not. His failure and frustration drove him to sign up as a sailor aboard the whaling ship *Acushet*. On January 3, 1841, he set sail for the South Seas.

ADVENTURES AND MISADVENTURES AT SEA

The ship's voyage was scheduled to last from 1841 to 1845. Melville finally was the world traveler he had always dreamed of becoming, seeing the sights of Brazil, Peru, Galapagos Islands, and the islands of the South Pacific. However, the whale hunting was not going well and as Captain Pease became more desperate, he also became crueler. He openly argued with his first and third mates, finally ordering them to leave the ship. Fed up with the conditions, Melville and fellow sailor Richard Tobias Greene deserted the ship on June 23, 1842, while anchored in the Marquesas Islands. The adventures that followed provided the basis for Melville's first novel, *Typee.*

Greene and Melville fled to the island's interior, planning to stay among the friendly Happa tribe. But the wild terrain proved more challenging than they had anticipated and they ended up in the territory of the Taipis (Typees), a fierce and unfriendly tribe rumored to be cannibals. Despite their reputation, the Taipis allowed the two sailors to live among them. But Melville, who was ill due to a leg injury, soon suspected they were more captives than guests. He became hopeful when Greene was allowed to leave in search of a doctor. When Greene never returned, Melville began to fear for his life. After a month, he escaped with the help of sailors from the Australian whaling ship, the *Lucy Ann.* Months later he learned that Greene had been captured and impressed aboard a whaler needing more crewmen. When Melville fictionalized his adventures in *Typee,* he described the setting as an Eden-like sanctuary from the encroaching aggressiveness of civilization.

On August 9, 1842, Melville joined the crew of the *Lucy Ann.* But his experience aboard this whaling ship was no better than it had been upon the last one. Several crewmen, including Melville, were put on trial for mutiny and imprisoned on Tahiti. He easily escaped and, along with John B. Troy, a demoted surgeon from the *Lucy Ann,* he explored life among the Tahitians and neighboring islands. These and subsequent adventures were later chronicled in his second novel, *Omoo.* He found Tahiti to be a paradise and would later write bitterly about outside civilization, especially missionaries, degrading the innocent Tahitian natives.

Paradise only held his attention for about a month before, in November of 1842, he signed on as a harpooner aboard the *Charles & Henry* out of Nantucket. Six months later he disembarked in Hawaii where he tried to get a job as a clerk and bookkeeper. In Hawaii he once again witnessed what he took to be debasement of natives by the so-called civilized intruders. He would write that the islanders had been "civilized into draft horses, and evangelized into beasts of burden." These sentiments were not popular at the time, decades before the Civil War, and contributed to keeping his books from becoming more popular.

Anxious to return home, on August 17, 1843, Melville enlisted as a seaman aboard the navy warship, the *United States*. The voyage to Boston took several months, during which several pivotal events occurred that would affect him deeply. First, his direct superior officer was John J. Chase, a charismatic leader with a love of literature, who became his close friend. Second, Herman's exposure to flogging on a navy ship (over 160 floggings were documented on that particular voyage) resulted in his later condemnation of its brutality and arbitrariness in *White-Jacket*. Third, during that trip he heard about the court-martial trial and subsequent hanging for mutiny of three Americans, one of whom was the son of the Secretary of War. The presiding judge was Melville's own cousin, Lieutenant Guert Gansevoort. This case became the inspiration for his final, and one of his most acclaimed novels, *Billy Budd*.

EARLY WRITING TRIUMPHS

In his absence, the family's fortunes had improved. Older brother Gansevoort had completed his law degree and was appointed secretary to the U.S. legation in London. Brother Allan was a successful Wall Street lawyer. The oldest sister Helen remained at home, but was often visited by her closest friend, Elizabeth Shaw, the daughter of Judge Lemuel Shaw of the Massachusetts Supreme Court. Melville delighted them all with his tales of adventure and was encouraged to write them down.

The result was his first novel, *Typee*. Harper and Brothers quickly rejected the book, finding the tales too outlandish. But Gansevoort had better luck in London, persuading publisher John Murray to print the book in England in 1846. An American edition followed. To everyone's surprise, the book was an immediate critical and financial success both in England and the United States. At twenty-six, Herman Melville had finally found a profession he both loved and was good at.

Melville's success was tempered with some bad news. Complaints rose about his negative depiction of missionaries as well as questions regarding the truthfulness of his idyllic descriptions of the natives and their way of life. In addition, Gansevoort died of a brain disease in May of 1846, leaving Melville now in charge of his family's finances. Despite the added responsibilities, Melville finished his second novel, *Omoo*, by the end of the year. *Omoo* continued where *Typee* had left off, and upon its publication in 1847, it also became a critical and financial success. Though most everyone agreed that Melville was an inspired and accomplished writer, still some voices persisted in criticizing his harsh treatment of missionaries.

Unfortunately, the success of the two novels was not enough to create a secure financial future, something that was especially important to Melville, given not only his impoverished past but his marriage in 1847 to his sister's friend, Elizabeth Shaw. In order to obtain some financial security, he petitioned for an appointment as a clerk in the U.S. Treasury Department in Washington. He was denied. Over the next twenty years he would continue to seek security through a job with the federal government, and he would continue to be denied.

THE FAMILY MAN

In 1847, Melville immersed himself in his new novel, *Mardi*. He was so determined that this book would be a literary departure from his earlier works that he instructed his publisher to refrain from even mentioning *Typee* and *Omoo*. During this time he became friendly with Evert Duyckinck, one of the editors at his publishing house, who introduced him to New York City's artistic and intellectual circles. Melville wrote reviews for Duyckinck's *Literary World* and helped start a comic magazine called *Yankee Doodle*.

Despite sharing a house with his brother Allan and Allan's wife, his mother and unmarried sisters, the years 1847 and 1848 were a very productive and happy time for Melville. Not only was his writing going well, but also his first child, Malcolm, was born. However, his increased responsibilities as a father put more pressure on him to be successful. Unfortunately, when *Mardi* was published in 1849, the reception was disastrous. Rather than continue his straightforward style of telling adventure stories, he had turned his third novel into an allegorical quest for the meaning of the universe. Critics and fans alike rejected this attempt and advised him to return to his former style.

Melville was devastated by the harsh reception of a book he was sure would not only continue his streak of success but elevate him as a literary writer. *Mardi*'s failure left him in financial difficulties and he was forced to churn out two adventure novels that would meet the expectations of his reading public. Published in 1849, *Redburn* was based on his first sailing trip aboard the *St. Lawrence*, while *White-Jacket*, published in 1850, details life aboard a man-of-war, including abuses in the U.S. Navy, similar to his experiences aboard the *United States*.

Both novels restored his reputation, but only as a writer of exciting adventure stories. But Melville wanted to be appreciated for his larger intellectual and literary designs. The perceptive reader of these latest novels could see a darker, more melancholy voice emerging. Though he had at one time embraced the optimistic views on the goodness of human nature of transcendentalist Ralph Waldo Emerson, his close reading of William Shakespeare's tragedies was giving his writing a more cynical and pessimistic edge.

THE WRITING OF *MOBY-DICK*

Most Melville scholars agree that perhaps the single most influential event in transforming Melville from the aspiring literary writer into the accomplished genius who produced *Moby-Dick* took place in 1850, when Duyckinck introduced him to Nathaniel Hawthorne, author of the acclaimed novel *Scarlet Letter*. Hawthorne was living in Pittsfield, the small town where Melville had spent time on his uncle's farm. Shortly thereafter, Melville moved his family to a nearby farm that he named "Arrowhead." The close proximity to one of the intellectual icons of American culture inspired Herman to take his own writing to a higher literary level.

Melville had promised his publisher he would deliver his new novel, first called *The Whale* and later titled *Moby-Dick*, by the fall of 1850. Before meeting with Hawthorne, he had described the proposed novel to his publisher as a "romance of adventure founded upon certain wild legends of the Southern Sperm Whale Fisheries, and illustrated by the author's own personal experience, of two years or more, as a harpooner." However, his friendship with Hawthorne helped change his vision of what the novel was about. He became less interested in the romantic adventure aspect and more involved in the philosophical and psychological exploration of human nature and our place in a seemingly uncaring universe.

More than his literary aspirations were riding on the publication of *Moby-Dick*. Melville's continuing struggle with finances had worsened. He'd borrowed $6,500 from his father-in-law in order to purchase Arrowhead, and he had borrowed from other sources at substantial interest rates. After several advances against royalties yet to be earned, his publisher refused to give him any more money. His first six novels had earned him only an average of about $1,200 each, not that much, even for his time, so *Moby-Dick* had to be a huge success or Melville risked plunging his family into the same sort of financial misfortune as his father had done.

The publication of *Moby-Dick* in 1851 did not produce the hoped-for acclaim or money. Reviews were mixed, though mostly negative, and sales were modest. Melville took some comfort in the glowing praise he received from Hawthorne. However, shortly after publication Hawthorne moved away, first to Concord, then to England as the American consul, and the friends grew apart, barely communicating with each other.

STRUGGLES FOR FINANCIAL SECURITY

Desperate for money, Melville plunged into his next novel, *Pierre*, confident he could produce another popular book, as he had done previously after the failure of *Mardi*. This novel, he assured Hawthorne's wife, would be "a rural bowl of milk" suitable for female readers, which he felt *Moby-Dick*, with its masculine cast and detailed brutality, had not been. Though he set out to imitate the novel of country life that was popular at the time in England and America, he ended up with a much darker, more intense exploration of human frailty and alienation than he had intended. The result was another critical and financial failure. Richard Bentley, his longtime British publisher, refused to print the book; Evert Duyckinck, his editor and friend, condemned the novel as the scribblings of a madman, thereby ending their friendship. Herman Melville, only thirty-three years old, was already washed up as a writer.

Worried about his obvious declining health as a result of long hours of writing, friends and relatives advised him to give up his literary pursuits altogether. They even tried to secure a consular appointment for him, though unsuccessfully. Though Melville's financial situation was indeed precarious, he was by no means verging on poverty. His wife had a small income from a trust fund, the farm made modest profits, and his writing, if not as rewarding as he hoped, still brought in some money.

Melville abandoned writing for a while in order to get his 160-acre farm back in working order. This was important, especially after the failure of *Pierre*, because the family received some of its income from the crops they produced. Fields were plowed and buildings repaired. But the lure of writing drew him back and between 1853 and 1855, he wrote several stories for periodicals, including "Bartleby the Scrivner" (1853), "The Encantadas" (1854), and "Benito Cereno" (1855). These dark stories reflected his own sense of despair and isolation. Though today they are considered masterpieces of the short story form and are anthologized worldwide, at the time they did little to enhance his career as a writer. Melville confessed in a letter to Hawthorne, "What I feel most moved to write will not pay."

While continuing to write magazine pieces that satirized the hypocrisies of society, Melville plunged into work on the novel *The Confidence-Man*, about a con man who cheats passengers during a steamer trip down the Mississippi River. Published in 1857, it was his last novel to appear during his lifetime. Ill health and financial pressures forced Melville to sell half of Arrowhead in April of 1856, for $5,500, although he still kept eighty acres of cleared fields, woods, and gardens. The following month his collected short works were published as *The Piazza Tales*.

Herman's wife Lizzie, tired of their isolation in the country and fearing for her husband's health, borrowed a large sum of money from her father against her eventual inheritance. She used the money to send Herman, now thirty-seven, on a long-desired voyage to the Mediterranean and the Holy Land. Privately, she expressed the hope that when he returned he would abandon writing, to which he had given so much and received so little. On October 11, 1856, he set sail aboard the steamer *Glasgow*, carrying with him a copy of *The Confidence-Man*, which he hoped to sell abroad.

TRAVELS ABROAD

His first stop was in England, where he visited with his old mentor and neighbor, Hawthorne. The visit was brief, due to Mrs. Hawthorne's illness, but the two men were able to rekindle their friendship within a few days. In his personal journal, Hawthorne noted how little his friend had changed over the years, still anxious for religious and philosophical discussions, still very somber in manner, and still completely lacking fashion sense in clothing. But still a good and moral man. "If he were a religious man," Hawthorne wrote, "he would be one of the most truly religious and reverential; he has a very high and noble nature, and better worth immortality than most of us."

Melville left for Turkey, then visited Greece and Malta, finally arriving in Egypt. With great effort he climbed the pyramids. The view from the top filled him, he said, with the sense of ageless and brooding mystery. By January of 1857 he was traveling through the Holy Land. He found Jerusalem more barren and less inspirational than he'd hoped and quickly returned to Greece. He toured several other European countries before returning to England for a final visit with Hawthorne, who, in Melville's absence, had arranged for the British publication of *The Confidence-Man*. On May 5, 1857, seven months after embarking on his voyage, Melville boarded the *City of Manchester* for his trip home.

FURTHER ISOLATION

Melville's return was marked with an elaborate party thrown by his father-in-law. Several literary giants were in attendance, including Richard Henry Dana Jr., author of the popular sea novel *Two Years Before the Mast*, and Oliver Wendell Holmes, a respected poet who was about to launch a new literary journal, the *Atlantic Monthly*. Melville seemed ready and eager to renew his writing career.

However, Melville's fortunes continued to worsen. *The Confidence-Man* turned out to be another critical and financial disaster. His American publisher went out of business, leaving him without a publisher and very poor prospects of getting another one. To make money, he began a series of lecture tours, beginning with the topic "Statues of Rome," for which he was paid an average of fifty dollars a lecture. His next lecture tour was on "The South Seas," billing himself as "the man who had lived among the cannibals." His family was pleased because there was more prestige in being a popular lecturer than an unsuccessful novelist. Friends commented that he seemed healthier and more energetic than he had in years. He was even writing another book, though not a novel this time but a book of poetry.

His third lecture tour, on "Traveling," proved less successful and Melville rattled around the house with nothing much to do but dwell on his declining health. Again his family encouraged him to take to the sea. In May of 1860, he set sail on the clipper ship *Meteor*, which was captained by his brother Thomas. Before leaving he signed over all his holdings to his wife's father, Judge Shaw, in exchange for cancellation of his debts. The judge agreed, immediately putting all the holdings in Lizzie's name. Melville also gave his book of poems to his brother Allan, asking him to seek a publisher while Melville was gone. Though the voyage was pleasant enough, he became restless and homesick, returning after six months, much earlier than expected. His arrival home didn't help his mood: Allan had been unable to find a publisher for his poems.

Again, he sought the stability of a government position, hoping he could arrange a consular appointment under the newly elected President Abraham Lincoln. Unfortunately, the death of his father-in-law sent him back to Boston. An inheritance gave the Melville's their first taste in a long time of financial security and they were able to live among friends in New York City instead of endure another bitter winter on the farm.

In April of 1861, the Civil War began. Melville volunteered to join the navy, but was turned down. In 1862, he decided to move to New York City permanently. While moving furniture, he suffered an accident that left him with cracked ribs and a broken shoulder blade. His recovery was painstakingly slow, leaving him often in dark moods. The next two years were spent redecorating his home in New York City, where he and his family lived a comfortable and socially active life. In 1864 he paid back a debt of two hundred dollars to Harper and Brothers for money they had advanced to him for earlier unsuccessful novels. This payment marked the end of his career as a novelist. From this point forward, he would publish mostly poetry.

In May of 1864, Herman learned of the death of his friend,

Hawthorne. This inspired him to memorialize their friendship in the poem "Monody":

> To have know him, to have loved him
>   After loneness long;
> And then to be estranged in life,
>   And neither in the wrong;
> And now for death to set his seal—
>   Ease me, a little ease, my song!

More poems followed, mostly about the Civil War, several of which were published in *Harper's*. Response was enthusiastic enough that in August of 1866, his collection of poems, *Battle-Pieces and Aspects of the War*, was published. Though they did call for better understanding between the North and the South, in general the poems were patriotic and not as controversial as many of his previous works. This may have helped Melville finally secure the government appointment he had sought for so many years. On December 5, 1866, at the age of forty-seven, he was sworn in as deputy inspector of customs for the port of New York, the first permanent salaried job of his life. The job was not physically or mentally demanding, allowing him plenty of time to continue his writing.

AN UNHAPPY FAMILY LIFE

Unfortunately, this period of financial security was also one of domestic insecurity and sadness. Lizzie was openly dissatisfied with her frequently moody husband. She was on the verge of seeking a legal separation when, in 1867, their eighteen-year-old son, Malcolm, died of a wound from his own pistol while alone in his bedroom. Whether the wound was self-inflicted or accidental is uncertain, but the result was to draw Melville and Lizzie closer together to endure the tragedy. But that closeness proved only temporary.

The family continued to deteriorate. Melville suffered from various ailments, one of which left him temporarily unable to use his hands. Lizzie, too, was stricken with a series of maladies, including severe hay fever. Their second son, Stanwix, followed the family tradition and went away to sea in 1869. Although one bright spot was the marriage of their younger daughter Francis in 1880, the older daughter Elizabeth experienced severe muscular rheumatism that threatened her life. Melville's brother died in 1884, followed by the death of Lizzie's brother a few weeks later. These tragic events took a deep toll on Melville, leaving him feeling tired and old. His one refuge, aside from writing, was gardening, and he often gave friends flowers from his well-tended garden.

During this time, several of his works—*Omoo, Redburn, White-Jacket,* and *Moby-Dick*—remained in print, gathering praise from younger writers in American and Britain. However, Melville's great literary ambition seemed to have left him at this stage of his life, and he was content to read, write, and garden. Several inheritances from Lizzie's side of the family left them with enough money that in 1885 Herman was able to quit his customs job after nineteen years of service. But the comfort of retirement was marred by the death of his son Stanwix far away in San Francisco after a long battle with tuberculosis.

THE LAST HURRAH

Herman continued to write poetry during his retirement. But his earlier fascination with the story he'd heard of a young sailor who'd been hanged for mutiny again captured his imagination and he began writing *Billy Budd,* which many critics believe to be, after *Moby-Dick,* his finest work. Ironically, no one knows for sure whether he ever finished writing the story. The version we have is dated April 19, 1891, but the manuscript is filled with revisions that suggest he was still working on it. Unfortunately, five months later, on September 28, he died of a heart attack at home, Lizzie at his side. The *New York Times* notice of his death mistakenly referred to him as Henry Melville.

Several years later, a Melville scholar researching the author discovered the manuscript in a tin box in the attic of Melville's home. When *Billy Budd* was finally published in 1924, the reaction was so strong that it prompted a Melville revival. *Moby-Dick* was once again being read and Herman Melville finally earned the reputation of literary genius that had eluded him during his lifetime.

CHARACTERS AND PLOT

CHARACTERS

Ishmael: The young, naïve sometime schoolteacher who, depressed with the meaninglessness of his life on land, decides to sign on as a sailor on a whaling ship, the *Pequod.* Ishmael is the narrator for most of the novel, revealing his opinions about all the crewmembers as well as about society, religion, and politics. However, he is not always a reliable narrator in that, although he tells the reader what he believes is the truth, the reader is aware that Ishmael is in fact wrong about many things.

Ahab: The captain of the *Pequod* once was a God-fearing pious husband and father who went whaling only to provide for his community. However, after losing his leg to Moby Dick (and rumored to have been struck by lightning), he has lost his faith that the world is overseen by a benevolent God. He chooses to hunt down the guilty whale, not to help his community, but to prove to himself that the universe is nothing more than a mechanistic natural order lacking any supernaturally imposed moral love of behavior. Ahab is sometimes demonic in his ruthless manipulation of his crew and sometimes angelic in his compassion for them, making him a complex tragic figure we are meant to both loathe and admire.

Moby Dick: More symbol than actual creature, the great white sperm whale takes on different meanings to different characters. The book contains several long passages detailing every bit of scientific information known about the sperm whale. Although these passages seem numbingly encyclopedic, and are often skipped by some readers, they are there to emphasize that it is impossible to know everything about a being, human or animal, just by knowing the scientific facts. The whales, as well as human beings, are greater than the sum of their body parts.

Starbuck: First mate of the *Pequod* and the on-board representative of staunch Christian moral values. Starbuck tries to fight Ahab's increasing megalomania by challenging the captain's motivations as well as actions. But, despite a good heart, he is no match for Ahab's powerful personality, and falls under Ahab's spell along with the others.

Stubb: Second mate of the *Pequod* and the on-board representative of the average working American. Stubb is well liked, a hard worker, and filled with good humor, but he refuses to look at anything beyond the superficial. He proclaims a trust in fate, and in doing so denies he has any responsibility in Ahab's destructive plan.

Flask: The no-nonsense, argumentative third mate on the *Pequod.*

Pip: Though only a lowly cabin boy on the *Pequod*, the young black boy becomes a pivotal character after he loses his sanity following an incident in which he is left alone, floating on the vast ocean for many hours. Melville deliberately uses this character to play the familiar Shakespearean archetype of the fool who, while saying things that other characters find hard to understand, is actually giving them key insights into their own characters as well as their futures.

Queequeg: Starbuck's harpooner, the dark-skinned, tattooed prince of a South Sea islander became a whaler in order to seek adventure. He represents not only the nontraditional native religions, which the novel suggests are as pertinent as Christianity, but also the intuitive "noble savage" part of a human being. Queequeg doesn't have to agonize about what is right or wrong, he knows inside. His character is meant to show how far removed civilization has become from this natural knowledge because we've replaced it with the overintellectualizing through science and theology. Throughout the voyage, Ishmael and Queequeg become closer friends, symbolizing not just Ishmael's overcoming racial prejudices, but embracing his own natural instincts about good and evil.

Tashtego: Stubb's harpooner and one of the few remaining members of the Gay Head tribe. He shares many of Queequeg's compassionate characteristics, defying common racial biases of the day.

Daggoo: Flask's physically imposing African harpooner.

Fedallah: Ahab's own harpooner, brought on board by Ahab for the sole purpose of killing Moby Dick. He is a fire-worshipping Parsee, meant to symbolize the demonic aspects of Ahab's quest.

Peleg: One of the wealthy owners of the *Pequod.*

Bildad: Peleg's partner in the ownership of the *Pequod.*

Father Mapple: The New Bedford preacher whose sermon about Jonah establishes the core thematic conflict of the novel. As a former whaler himself, he has experienced many trials, but has used those trials to embrace what he considers to be the wisdom and goodness of God, unlike Ahab, who sees his trials as proof that either there is no God or that God is evil.

PLOT SUMMARY

Aside from the 135 chapters and epilogue that are the main text of the story of the hunt for the great white sperm whale Moby Dick, the novel also contains two opening sections called Etymology and Extracts. The Etymology, compiled by a fictional "consumptive usher [assistant schoolmaster] to a grammar school," presents a variety of definitions of the word "whale" as well as the word translated into several languages. The Extracts, compiled by a fictional "sub-sub-librarian," offer dozens of brief excerpts about whales from both fiction and non-fiction. Many of the selections are from great literary writers, thereby demonstrating the enormous significance to humanity of the whale, in both mythology and commerce.

The narrator begins his story with three of the most famous words in literature: "Call me Ishmael." He quickly explains that the events he is about to relate took place some years ago, when he was a young man. Broke and without anything to interest him on shore, he decides to do what he usually does whenever "I find myself involuntarily pausing before coffin warehouses, and bringing up the rear of every funeral that I meet": go to sea in pursuit of adventure. He describes the people he sees wandering about New York City, believing that each person secretly shares his desire to abandon his mundane life on shore and go to sea. Ishmael makes it clear that there are several reasons he prefers going as a sailor rather than a passenger, the most important of which is that he gets paid for his troubles. With youthful sarcasm he explains that "The urbane activity with which a man receives money is really marvelous, considering that we so earnestly believe money to be the root of all earthly ills, and that on no account can a monied man enter heaven.

Ah! how cheerfully we consign ourselves to perdition."

Seeking a ship to join, Ishmael arrives at the whaling port of New Bedford, Massachusetts, on a Saturday night in December. Too late to catch the ferry to Nantucket, where the more traditional whaling ships are, he is forced to stay over a few days in New Bedford. Unable to afford one of the better inns, he comes across the dismal run-down Spouter-Inn whose sign emits a "forlorn creaking" and whose owner is named Peter Coffin, ominous portents that Ishmael recognizes but overlooks because the place looks cheap. However, the inn is crowded and Ishmael's only option is to share a room—and bed—with a black harpooner from the South Seas named Queequeg, who, Peter Coffin informs Ishmael, is out selling shrunken heads.

Ishmael awaits the arrival of Queequeg with great trepidation. When the harpooner finally arrives, Ishmael pretends to be asleep while he watches the tall, tattooed man go through rituals of worshiping a small, dark idol, Yojo. When Queequeg finally discovers the cowering Ishmael, he raises his tomahawk-pipe. Ishmael's screams bring Peter Coffin, who explains the situation to Queequeg, who then retires to the bed. Ishmael also turns in and "never slept better in my life."

The next day, Ishmael marvels at Queequeg's "civilized manners," as he watches the harpooner dress himself in fancy clothes and shave himself with his harpoon. Ishmael sets out to see the sights of New Bedford, a town made wealthy from the whaling industry. He enters the Whaleman's Chapel, where "few are the moody fisherman, shortly bound for the Indian Ocean or Pacific, who fail to make a Sunday visit to the spot." In another moment of foreboding, he begins reading the many memorials to dead and lost sailors that are masoned into the wall. Ishmael's reaction is at first fear: "Yes, there is death in this business of whaling—a speechlessly quick chaotic bundling of a man into Eternity." But almost immediately he feels merry, thinking that at least death on a ship will bring him the same immortality as these other dead sailors whose names are forever embedded in the walls of the chapel. He unexpectedly finds idol-worshipping Queequeg at the chapel.

Finally, the chapel's brooding but charismatic minister, Father Mapple, ascends a rope ladder to the pulpit, which is designed to look like the bow of a ship. Mapple's sermon reflects on the meaning of the biblical tale of Jonah, who was swallowed by what has been interpreted as a whale. He warns of the devastating price to be paid for disobeying God's will. "With the sin of disobedience in him, Jonah still further flouts at God, by seeking to flee from him," Mapple says, articulating Ishmael's own internal conflict and foreshadowing the conflicts Ishmael will soon face. Mapple's emotional sermon leaves him exhausted and kneeling on the pulpit in a pose of humility as the worshipers depart.

Upon returning to the Spouter-Inn following the sermon, Ishmael observes Queequeg in the act of worshiping his idol and concludes, "You cannot hide the soul. Through all unearthly tattooings, I thought I saw traces of a simple honest heart. . . ." Thus, the two become best friends, with Ishmael even participating in a smoking ritual that "marries" them. As a result of their new relationship, Queequeg gives half of his belongings to Ishmael, while Ishmael politely worships Queequeg's idol. They end the day by climbing into bed together and chatting. "Thus, then, in our hearts' honeymoon," rhapsodizes Ishmael, "lay I and Queequeg—a cosy, loving pair." During this time, Queequeg recounts his childhood on the South Pacific island of Kokovoko, where he was the king's son. Anxious for adventure, he stowed away on a ship and eventually was allowed to become a whaler. He tells Ishmael that he can never return home because his exposure to Christianity would be considered a defilement.

Ishmael and Queequeg leave for Nantucket. On the ferry, a group of young men mimic Queequeg, who promptly snags one of them, and nonchalantly flips him around in a somersault, dropping him on the deck. As the captain is rebuking Queequeg, the ferry's boom knocks the dazed young man overboard. Queequeg dives over and rescues him, afterward receiving praise from all aboard, including the captain.

Once they arrive in Nantucket, they take a room at the Try-Pot, owned by Peter Coffin's cousin. Queequeg says his idol Yojo insists that Ishmael select the ship for both of them, which turns out to be the *Pequod.* Ishmael negotiates his lay (portion of the profits from the whales they kill) with two of the ship's owners, Bildad and Peleg, Quakers who seemingly contradict their religious beliefs by being both cheap when paying the crew and by trafficking in the slaughter of whales. Ishmael discovers that the *Pequod*'s captain is Ahab, well respected but reclusive since the great white sperm whale, Moby Dick, "devoured, chewed up, crunched" his leg.

At first, Bildad and Peleg don't want Queequeg on the ship because he's a pagan. But as soon as Queequeg accurately hurls his harpoon at a small bit of tar on the water, they immediately sign him up, giving him a generous ninetieth lay, more than any other harpooner has ever been given out of Nantucket. In contrast, Ishmael was offered only a three hundredth lay. Following signing on, Ishmael and Queequeg are approached by a "beggar-like stranger" named Elijah, a self-proclaimed prophet whose face is scarred from smallpox. He warns them that their souls are in peril if they ship out with Ahab, but Ishmael pronounces him "a humbug" and ignores him. A few days later, when the ship is stocked with provisions and Ahab is recovered from losing his leg, the *Pequod* sets sail on Christmas day. Ominous forebodings continue as Peleg and Bildad, not the still-unseen Ahab, pilot the ship out of port. After the owners return to shore, the crew gives "three heavy-hearted cheers, and blindly plunged like fate into the lone Atlantic."

During the first part of the voyage, Ishmael ruminates on both the possibility of death at sea and of the significance of whales and whaling to civilization. While watching the sailor Bulkington steer the ship, Ishmael concludes that the man is fated to die at sea, a death that ennobles him much more than the ignoble death of a coward. For the sailors on a whaling ship are bravely providing for the rest of civilization, both in terms of economics and knowledge.

Ishmael quickly assesses the three main officers of the *Pequod*. He finds Starbuck, the thirty-year-old first mate, descended from Quakers, to be moral and cautious, with a healthy respect for and fear of nature, especially as embodied by whales: "'I will have no man in my boat,' said Starbuck, 'who is not afraid of a whale.'" Having lost his own father and brother to whaling, Starbuck does not wish to foolishly risk lives. This respectful attitude also reflects his Christian convictions that humans must be humble in the presence of God's power, of which whales are a manifestation. Stubb, the second mate, is happy-go-lucky, neither seeking danger nor shying away from it: "Good-humored, easy, and careless, he presided over his whale-boat as if the most deadly encounter were but a dinner, and his crew all invited guests." Third mate Flask is a no-nonsense man who is "very pugnacious concerning whales, who somehow seemed to think that the great Leviathans had personally and hereditarily affronted him; and therefore it was sort of a point of honor with him to destroy them whenever encountered." Each officer commands a whale boat, a small vessel from which the whale is attacked and killed. Each whale boat has its own harpooner: Starbuck's is Queequeg; Stubb's is Tashtego, a Gay Head Indian; Flask's is the African Daggoo, "a gigantic, coal-black negro-savage, with a lion-like tread." Ishmael also notes the presence of Pip, the "poor Alabama Boy" who stands on the "grim Pequod's forecastle" and plays the tambourine. From his observations of the international crew, Ishmael somewhat sarcastically concludes that while the "American liberally provides the brains, the rest of the world as generously suppl[ies] the muscles."

Finally, Ishmael sees the elusive Captain Ahab, who looks "like a man cut away from the stake, when the fire has overrunningly wasted all the limbs without consuming them." Ahab stands firm on his peg leg made from the jaw of a whale, his face and body ravaged from his encounter with Moby Dick. Already Ishmael can see the unrelenting determination in Ahab's gaze as he stares out over the prow looking into the distance: "There was an infinity of firmest fortitude, a determinate, unsurrenderable wilfulness, in the fixed and fearless, forward dedication of that glance."

Ahab's troubled mind is reflected in his harsh treatment of Stubb, whom he calls a dog, as well as his restless pacing of the ship. Even his soothing habit of pipe-smoking fails to help, so he tosses his pipe overboard and continues pacing the deck. The next morning Ahab commands the crew to be alert for whales and "If ye see a white one, split your lungs for him!"

The narrative is interrupted by a couple chapters of Ishmael ruminating on the "science of whales" as discussed in literature as well as on the whaling industry itself. He also reflects on Ahab's demeanor as a captain, finding him to be unremarkable. Although he searches for something grand in the man, he concludes that such a characteristic must be "plucked at from the skies, and dived for in the deep," another foreshadowing of events to come.

Ishmael is sent to the watch for whales on the masthead, at the top of the masts. Here he ruminates on the dangers one faces on watch. Not only is the perch uncomfortable, but also a sailor who stares too long at the sea could be "lulled into such an opium-like listlessness of vacant, unconscious reverie . . . that at last he loses his identity." The dangers of losing one's identity at sea are even more emphasized when Ahab appears to whip his crew into a whale-hunting frenzy, abandoning all sense of who they were in order to adopt their charismatic captain's quest. Ahab's skillful manipulation of the men is accomplished both through speech and avarice. He mesmerizes them with his charisma, vowing to chase Moby Dick "round perdition's flames before I give him up." And he offers a Spanish gold doubloon to the first man to spy Moby Dick. Only Starbuck questions the reasonableness of his captain's quest, but even he is powerless before Ahab. Following a communion-like ceremony in which Ahab has his harpooners, "my three pagan kinsmen," remove their spearheads and drink from them, the crew belongs to Ahab, both in hearts and minds.

Afterward, Ahab, Starbuck, and Stubb go their separate ways, each revealing through a monologue their reaction to what just happened as well as to the quest ahead. Ahab watches the sunset and ruminates on his own "demoniac" attitude, yet remains convinced that he is fated to hunt and kill Moby Dick. Starbuck acknowledges his own sense of duty in helping Ahab, even though he suspects it will lead to doom. Stubb's attitude is that life is fated and therefore "a laugh's the wisest, easiest answer."

Ishmael's thoughts during the next part of the voyage turn to Moby Dick as he ruminates on the rise in reported whale attacks and meaning of whale's whiteness, concluding that he has "great ferocity, cunning, and malice." At the same time, Ishmael decides that Ahab's apparent madness in his obsession over Moby Dick is due to lack of medical care during the long voyage home after losing his leg. When Tashtego finally sights a whale, Ishmael suddenly spies Ahab "surrounded by five dusky phantoms that seemed fresh formed out of air." This is the secret whaling crew that Ahab has hidden in the cargo hold, keeping them isolated from the rest of the crew. Their leader is the harpooner Fedallah, who wears a turban and a Chinese jacket and who is "tall and swart, with one white tooth evilly protruding from its steel-like lips." The others are dark-skinned men from the Philippines.

The boats are lowered and the men pursue the whale. Queequeg alone sticks the whale with his harpoon, but the wounded mammal capsizes the boat. An eerie mist covers the water, resulting in the *Pequod* nearly killing the men it is searching for. Finally they are rescued. The incident reminds Ishmael of his own mortality, prompting him to write a will, with Queequeg's help. He admits that this is the fourth time as a sailor he has done so, as making wills is a popular pastime among sailors. Ishmael also wonders at Ahab's decision to captain his own whaling boat with Fedallah and his men, thereby risking the commercial purpose of the voyage.

Ishmael's concern is heightened when, after enduring a difficult trip around Africa's southern tip, the Cape of Good Hope, they pass a ship called the *Albatross*. Ahab questions the captain about the whereabouts of Moby Dick, but the wind yanks the speaking trumpet from the captain's mouth and the ship continues on silently. Ishmael worries that their voyage may be nothing more than a meaningless circle that takes them "only through numberless perils to the very point whence we started." The meeting with the *Albatross* inspires Ishmael to tell a story he'd heard about another ship, the *Town-Ho*, supposedly from one of the principals, a sailor named Steelkilt. Steelkilt led a mutiny against a mate named Radney. The mutineers were eventually caught and flogged, but Steelkilt wanted revenge against Radney for the flogging. However, in the process of trying to harpoon Moby Dick, Radney was knocked out of the boat. The whale snatched him up and "plunged headlong again, and went down." This casts a deeper ominous tone over the *Pequod*'s mission.

The whale boats pursue what they think is Moby Dick but turns out to be only a giant squid. However, they spot a sperm whale, give chase, and kill it. Though whalemen in general don't eat whale meat, Stubb demands that Daggoo go overboard and cut him a whale steak. He then orders the black cook, Fleece, to make him supper from the whale meat. While eating, Stubb is annoyed at the sound of the sharks feeding on the whale. He admonishes Fleece to "go and preach to 'em" the importance of moderation and civility. Fleece delivers a sermon to the sharks that thinly equates human nature with the sharkish feeding frenzy. He tells them that the fact that they have big mouths doesn't mean they have big bellies and that they should use those big mouths to bite off blubber for the smaller sharks. Stubb responds enthusiastically with "Well done, Fleece! . . . That's Christianity. . . ."

Another whale is killed at night and lashed to the ship to be processed in the morning. However, the sharks attack the whale with such ferocity that the crew must battle them most of the night. Queequeg's hand is almost severed by the teeth of a dead shark they've hauled aboard. Afterward, Ishmael details the processing of the whale, its "funeral," and the whale's beheading. As the men eat their meal, Ahab converses with the whale's head dangling from the ship's side, asking it what wonders and terrors it has witnessed.

An encounter with another ship, the *Jeroboam*, provokes even more foreboding. Because of an epidemic aboard, Captain Mayhew of the *Jeroboam* speaks to Ahab from a small boat aside the *Pequod*. With him is the self-proclaimed archangel Gabriel, who had warned the captain against pursuing Moby Dick. His advice was ignored when they came across Moby Dick a year later, which resulted in the death of a crewman. The rest of the crew had, as a result, become his followers. Captain Mayhew asks Ahab if he still intends to pursue Moby Dick, to which Ahab responds simply, "Aye." Gabriel instantly springs to his feet and, pointing downward, exclaims, "Think, think of the blasphemer—dead, and down there!—beware the blasphemer's end!"

A right whale is killed and, at Fedallah's suggestion, the head is mounted on the opposite side of the ship. Ishmael offers much information about the physical characteristics of each whale head. One part of the whale's head is the case, which the sailors set about taking the sperm from. During this operation, Tashtego plummets into the case, which is at least twenty feet deep. A rescue attempt fails, causing the head to break free from the ship and drop into the ocean. Queequeg dives in and saves Tashtego, delivering him "with great skill in obstetrics" from the head of the whale like a baby.

The *Pequod* encounters a German whaling ship, the *Jungfrau* (Virgin), whose crew has been so unsuccessful at capturing whales they have to borrow oil. Suddenly whales are spotted and both ships give chase. The *Pequod* kills an old whale, which they lash to the side of the ship. However, the ancient whale begins to sink, pulling the *Pequod* under and it must be cut loose.

Once again, Ishmael ponders the mysteries of the whale, this time considering its role in mythology and religion. He reconsiders the biblical story of Jonah that Father Mapple had discussed, offering scientific reasons why a man could not survive inside a whale as well as theological arguments against scientific reasoning. Ishmael's ruminations are interrupted when they chase a "grand Armada" of whales and are in turn chased by pirates. They elude the pirates and manage to kill one whale. Afterward, Ishmael explains to the reader more about the behavior of whales and fishing laws of England.

The *Pequod* comes across a French ship, called the *Bouton de Rose* (Rose-Bud). Its name is ironic because the ship, due to the fact that it has two dead whales strapped to it, produces "a peculiar and not very pleasant smell." Stubb dupes the inexperienced captain into cutting free one of the whales because it has no oil. What Stubb does not tell the captain is that the whale's bowels contain ambergris, which is made into perfume. Stubb pretends to do the captain a favor by hauling away the carcass, only to harvest six handfuls of the ambergris for the *Pequod*. Ahab grows impatient with the delay and warns Stubb to abandon the whale and come aboard or be left behind.

The young, black cabin boy Pip replaces an oarsman on Stubb's whaling boat. The first time he does a good job. But the second time, when a whale taps the boat, Pip leaps out in fear, which causes them to lose the whale. Stubb warns Pip not to do that again. When Pip does leap out again, Stubb leaves him behind as a lesson. Though only alone for an hour, the experience leaves Pip wandering "about the deck an idiot." But Ishmael believes Pip saw wondrous things and "so man's insanity is heaven's sense; and wandering from all mortal reason, man comes at last to that celestial thought, which, to reason, is absurd and frantic. . . ."

The crew sets about to process the whale, taking the spermaceti from its head and the blubber from its body. Ishmael is moved by the act of all the men squeezing the lumpy sperm into liquid and sees it as a communal act of brotherhood. However, the try-works, with all its boiling cauldrons for boiling oil from blubber, reminds him of funeral pyres and hell. His good will from the sperm-squeezing is replaced by a dread that he has lost his moral compass of what is right and wrong.

Ishmael, Ahab, Starbuck, Stubb, Flask, and the Manxman (a sailor who comes from the English Isle of Man) each react to the gold doubloon that Ahab has nailed to the mainmast as a reward for spotting Moby Dick. Each interprets the coin differently, revealing his own interpretation of the world. Pip mutters crazily, warning that "it's a sign that things grow desperate," and that Moby Dick will nail Ahab.

An English whaling ship, the *Samuel Enderby*, encounters the *Pequod*. The ship's captain, Boomer, has lost an arm chasing Moby Dick. But rather than dwell on the loss by taking it as a personal affront, like Ahab, Captain Boomer is happy to be alive. In fact, when Moby Dick had appeared again, he had refused to chase it, having learned his lesson. Ahab, rather than learning from Boomer's experience, only cares about interrogating the captain concerning Moby Dick's location. When he has it, he begins the chase again.

When the oil casks are found to be leaking, Starbuck suggests to Ahab that they stop the chase in order to fix them. Ahab denies the request. When Starbuck protests, Ahab threatens him with a musket. Starbuck warns Ahab to beware of himself. Ahab then agrees to stop to fix the casks, acknowledging, "Though art but too good a fellow, Starbuck."

Queequeg falls ill and, thinking he is dying, orders his coffin to be made. He places his harpoon, idol, and other precious possessions in it and climbs inside with them. However, he soon regains his health through, he claims, his own willpower. Afterward, he uses his coffin as a locker for his worldly goods. He copies the tattoos from his body, the work of a prophet from his tribe, onto the coffin lid.

In anticipation of finding Moby Dick, Ahab directs the blacksmith to forge a new harpoon. But Ahab soon takes over the task, hammering the glowing rods "and bowing over his head towards the fire, seemed invoking some curse or some blessing on the toil." To complete this hellish imagery, Melville has Ahab tempering the hot metal, not with water, but with blood from the three harpooners. Ahab now paces the deck with his newly fashioned ivory leg and blood-christened harpoon while Pip's "wretched laugh" echoes about the ship.

The *Pequod* meets a Nantucket whaler, the *Bachelor*, whose happy crew is celebrating as they return home with a full cargo. Ahab declines an invitation to join the celebration, wanting only news of Moby Dick. The captain replies that, though he's heard stories of the great whale, he doesn't believe them. Ahab continues his search.

One night Fedallah prophesizes his own death as well as Ahab's. He proclaims that before Ahab dies he will see two hearses, "the first not made by mortal hands; and the visible wood of the last one must be grown in America." Ahab dismisses the prophecy since he can't imagine seeing hearses at sea. Fedallah announces that he will die before Ahab, but will pilot him still. Ahab dismisses this, too, vowing that "I have here two pledges that I shall yet slay Moby Dick and survive it." Fedallah continues with his prophecies, declaring that Ahab will be killed by hemp. Ahab interprets this to mean being hanged, which he also dismisses by proclaiming, "I am immortal then, on land and on sea."

A typhoon hits the *Pequod*, destroying one of the harpoon boats. Lightning threatens the three masts, but rather than erect lightning rods, Ahab marvels in the sight. Starbuck and Ahab argue about safety procedures. That night, Starbuck considers assassinating Ahab, but cannot bring himself to do it. The next morning the compasses are found to be faulty due to the storm. Ahab then fashions his own compass from the head of his lance. The crew watches in awe as Ahab's compass does indeed point properly, to which Ahab exclaims, "Look ye, for yourselves, if Ahab be not the lord of the level loadstone." The crew marvels at Ahab's compass and one by one "they slunk away." Ishmael studies Ahab, observing that "In his fiery eyes of scorn and triumph, you then saw Ahab in all his fatal pride." But that pride is tempered with compassion as Ahab takes pity on Pip and has him stay in the captain's cabin, cementing their friendship as well as intertwining their fates.

When a crewman falls from the mast, a life buoy is thrown over to save him. However, the old, dried buoy quickly sinks and the crewman drowns. The mates order the carpenter to adapt Queequeg's coffin as a life buoy.

The *Rachel* approaches the *Pequod*. Captain Gardiner explains that his son was lost during a chase after Moby Dick and begs Ahab to help them search for him. But Ahab refuses, preferring instead to continue the hunt for Moby Dick. Anxious about the impending meeting with the white whale, Ahab spends more time pacing the deck. Not wishing to be distracted by compassion for Pip, he orders the cabin boy to remain in the cabin. Nor is Ahab distracted by seeming omens of doom, such as when he climbs the mast to look for Moby Dick and a black hawk steals his hat. Or when they encounter another whaling ship, the *Delight*, which is limping home after an encounter with Moby Dick, even dumping a body overboard as the *Pequod* sails by.

Finally, Ahab himself sights Moby Dick. All the whale boats give chase, with Ahab's own boat being destroyed and the crew thrown into the water. Starbuck saves them by steering the *Pequod* after the whale, chasing it away. The next day three harpoon boats give chase again, and again Moby Dick defeats them. This time he destroys Flask and Stubb's boats and capsizes Ahab's boat. During the encounter, Ahab's new whale-bone leg breaks in two. Ahab returns to the ship to learn that Fedallah is dead, dragged down by Moby Dick after becoming entangled in a harpoon line. Fedallah's prophecy that he would die before Ahab comes true. Starbuck once again tries to convince Ahab to abandon the hunt, but Ahab refuses.

On the third day, Ahab prepares to give chase again. He and Starbuck exchange a moment of camaraderie in which the first mate tearfully begs Ahab not to go: "Oh, my captain, my captain—noble heart—go not—go not. . . ." Ahab goes anyway. Moby Dick rises "bedraggled with trailing ropes, and harpoons, and lances" and damages two of the boats with his flailing tail. Only Ahab remains "almost without a scar." Ahab sees Fedallah's dead body lashed to Moby Dick and recognizes the fulfillment of Fedallah's prophecy of the appearance of a hearse, with the whale acting as a hearse.

Moby Dick dives out of sight. When they spot him again they give chase. This time the whale swims straight for the *Pequod*, stoving in the hull and sinking it. Ahab recognizes the ship to be the second hearse, made of American wood and transporting its cargo of dead bodies. With renewed vigor and vengeance, Ahab attacks Moby Dick, with his harpoon. The whale lurches and the hemp line attached to the harpoon catches Ahab around the neck—as in Fedallah's prophecy—and Ahab is "shot out of the boat, ere the crew knew he was gone." The sinking *Pequod* creates a powerful vortex that drags the rest of the ships and crew under the water and out of sight.

Ishmael is the lone survivor, having been thrown clear of the area. He manages to cling to the floating coffin of Queequeg until he is rescued the next day by the *Rachel*, which "in her retracing search after her missing children, only found another orphan."

CHAPTER 1

The Art of *Moby-Dick*

Melville's Style Is Both Original and a Reflection of His Times

Richard Chase

Richard Chase demonstrates how Melville's style uses techniques familiar to readers of that time, but is also deliberately innovative. Grand oratory was a popular style in Melville's time and Chase shows how Melville parodies it, thereby parodying the values that it represents. Melville then creates his own unique style through powerful imagery. Richard Chase was professor of English at Columbia University and the author of many books on American literature, including *Walt Whitman Reconsidered* and *The American Novel and Its Traditions*.

It is clear by now that whatever may be said for or against Melville's style, he was a consciously "literary" writer, not, as used to be said, an unlettered or "natural" genius. [Nineteenth-century American novelist] Henry James, it could once be said, was a "literary" writer, whereas Melville was simply a great talent with no special professional sense of his medium. We can now see that Melville was fully as "literary" as James, if by "literary" we mean conscious of style (which is not to imply that Melville is the equal of James as a stylist).

Melville had other models of style besides the great English authors. One of these was the popular American rhetoric and oratory of his own time. And whereas this accounts for much of what one objects to in Melville's prose—its occasional clumsiness, its purposeless inflation, its vagueness, its jargon—it also accounts for many of his most felicitous passages. A glance at such a story as *The Obedient Wife*, written in 1840 by an anonymous author for the popular New York journal *Spirit of the Times*, will demonstrate how dependent Melville sometimes was on this sort of prose:

> There is an old story of a man who had married a young lady, and who had a friend somewhat skeptical as to the obedient tendency of the wife's disposition, much to the dissatisfaction of the Benedick, who strongly asserted, and warmly asseverated, that his will was law, and that she never by any chance disobeyed any wish or injunction of his.
>
> "Have you ever tried her in that respect?" said his friend.

There are long passages in Melville which sound just like this. It is, of course, very consciously literary. The writer feels that he would be less literary if he wrote "who had a friend somewhat skeptical of his wife's obedience" instead of "somewhat skeptical as to the obedient tendency of his wife's disposition." It is a genuine low-Melvillian trick; and so is the delicious reference to the "Benedick," the toying with "asserted" and "asseverated," and the magniloquent humor of "Have you ever tried her *in that respect?*" The following passage, also from the *Spirit of the Times,* might easily have been written by him who tells the story of *Typee* or *Omoo* or *Mardi.*

> When we got up and rubbed our eyes, to our great disappointment we found that neither day nor wind would suit for "*Snipe Shooting*", so we sat down to our salt shad and our rye coffee, as disconsolate as Israel's maids of yore beside Babylon's waters. Looking out on the glittering expanse of Shinnecock Bay, we gazed with feelings of envy on the clam-men at anchor in their graceful whaleboats, who never knew the *ennui* arising from want of occupation, and were now engaged in destroying the happiness of many a bivalve's family circle with their merciless rakes. . . . After dinner,—a repetition of our morning's enticing fare,—we sat down to enjoy a quiet smoke. "Pooh! Pish! Psha!" muttered L——, a stately old bachelor.
>
> "Damn the day," exclaimed B——, who was an irascible ditto, not reflecting for a moment that Providence would be unwilling to increase the torrid state of the air by adding the hyper-temperature of the infernal regions. As for myself I don't exactly remember what I did, but I believe I ejected a mouthful of smoke and whistled.

Truly Ishmaelian is the philosophical humorist who here ejects his mouthful of smoke. The writer of this passage is a very literary writer, highly conscious of his allusions, careful to use a French word, proud of saying "the hyper-temperature of the infernal regions." He is jocular, reflective, acutely conscious of words. Carefully he constructs a mask of rhetoric and places it between the reader and that which is being described, hiding or merely obscuring the truth behind his featureless style. Probably he is not aware that his style *is* featureless, that what he takes to be a rich humorous-serious involution of phrase is really, much of it, blank and meaningless jargon.

MELVILLE RECOGNIZES THE DANGERS OF GRAND ORATORY

There arose in this country in the 1830's and 1840's a most violent spirit of magniloquence. Oratory was one of the accomplishments of the folk hero. "I can outspeak any man," was one of [nineteenth-century frontiersman and politician Davy] Crockett's boasts. An orotund native oratory, full of bombast, humorous mythology, and rough Americanisms, emerged, as if by necessity, to express the tumultuous feelings of the people. This oratorical language, which could be heard in various forms in tall talk, in congressional addresses, in sermons and written literature, had its effect on Melville, as did the milder humorous jargon we have glanced at above. As [twentieth-century American humorist] H.L. Mencken observes, the native rhetoric had its influence on [nineteenth-century American poet Walt] Whitman and [nineteenth-century American writer] Mark Twain (he does not mention Melville), helping to set them apart from the conventional writers of the time, who looked back to the style of [eighteenth-century English writer Joseph] Addison and [eighteenth-century English writer Samuel] Johnson. The distinction must have been brought home to Melville in the 1850's, when he began to send short stories to literary magazines; one editor, distressed by Melville's style, suggested that he try to emulate Addison. . . .

The feeling of power, openness, space, and freedom is the central emotion in many of Melville's best passages, and as any reader of *Moby-Dick* will know, Melville purges the mood of exaltation of all vulgarities, of mere power worship, muscle-flexing, or intoxication with the *mystique* of force and space. . . . In [his earlier novel, *Mardi*,] he represents his travelers as stopping off in Washington to visit the Senate. They hear a speech by a senator from the West. Roaring like a wild beast and smiting his hip with one hand and his head with the other, the speaker proceeds thus (I substitute real names for Melville's mythical ones):

I have said it! the thunder is flashing, the lightning is crashing!

already there's an earthquake in England! Full soon will the King discover that his diabolical machinations against this ineffable land must soon come to naught. Who dare not declare that we are not invincible? I repeat it, we are. Ha! ha! The audacious King must bite the dust! . . . Ha! ha! I grow hoarse; but would mine were a voice like the wild bull's . . . that I might be heard from one end of this great and gorgeous land to its farthest zenith; ay, to the uttermost diameter of its circumference.

The felicity of Melville's parody indicates clearly enough that he was aware of the false and dangerous emotions lying beneath this kind of oratory—despite the fact that he was himself not entirely proof against the oratorical mood. This kind of "screaming" caused him many doubts about the American future and convinced him that America might be throwing away all the opportunities of its wonderful youth even as it enthusiastically celebrated its own newfound confidence. He saw two aspects of the American spirit. He feared, on the one hand, that America would never be more than the "braggadocio" of the world. He hoped, on the other hand, that America was like "St. John, feeding on locusts and honey, and with prophetic voice, crying to the nations from the wilderness." Both of these possibilities he detected in the rough and fulsome cadences of American speech.

In *Moby-Dick* the language of the screamer is transmuted, when Melville is at his best, into an exalted apostrophe to power, space, and freedom. The mood is at once lyric in its poignancy and epic in the large nobility of its vision. The mood is not brutal or blind or chaotic or megalomaniac. It is serene and joyful, with the serenity and joy which follow upon the sense of great power controlled and great violence purged. It is the mood expressed by Father Mapple at the end of his sermon (which is itself perhaps the high point of American oratory):

> Delight is to him—a far, far upward and inward delight— who against the proud gods and commodores of this earth, ever stands forth his own inexorable self. Delight is to him whose strong arms yet support him, when the ship of this base, treacherous world has gone down beneath him. Delight is to him who gives no quarter in the truth and kills, burns, and destroys all sin though he pluck it out from under the robes of Senators and Judges.

THE THREE STYLES OF *MOBY-DICK*

The style of *Moby-Dick* is a rhythm of three basic styles: the style of fact, the style of oratorical celebration of fact, the style of meditation moving toward mysticism. A passage from the chapter called "Nantucket" will document this:

> What wonder that these Nantucketers, born on a beach, should take to the sea for a livelihood! They first caught crabs and quohogs in the sand; grown bolder, they waded out with nets for mackerel; more experienced, they pushed off in boats and captured cod;

these are facts; but gradually the reader's attention is led away from fact toward a vision of size and power; the speech becomes metaphorical; the field of observation opens out:

> and at last, launching a navy of great ships on the sea, explored this watery world; put an incessant belt of circumnavigations around it; peeped in at Bering's Straits; and in all seasons and all oceans declared everlasting war with the mightiest animated mass that has survived the flood; most monstrous and most mountainous! That Himmalehan, salt-sea Mastodon, clothed with such portentousness of unconscious power, that his very panics are more to be dreaded than his most fearless and malicious assaults!

Note the quality of the images. The "incessant belt of circumnavigations" for size, and for the cyclical route of the voyager; "peeped in" for vision; "the flood," one of Melville's favorite symbols for the primal sense of power and space; "Himmalehan," image of the mountain; the "Mastodon" with his "portentousness of unconscious power," a phallic, imperial, and masculine image.

As the rhythm of the style turned upward and outward into space, Melville would have had the sensations he expressed in another chapter: "One often hears of writers that rise and swell with their subject, though it may seem but an ordinary one. How then with me, writing of this Leviathan? Unconsciously my chirography expands into placard capitals. Give me a condor's quill! Give me Vesuvius' crater for an inkstand! Friends, hold my arms!" And, then, Melville writing in full possession of his power, there follows the celebration of the Nantucketers:

> And thus have these naked Nantucketers, these sea hermits, issuing from their ant-hill in the sea, overrun and conquered the watery world like so many Alexanders parcelling out among them the Atlantic, Pacific, and Indian oceans, as the three pirate powers did Poland. Let America add Mexico to Texas, and pile Cuba upon Canada; let the English overswarm all India, and hang out their blazing banner from the sun; two thirds of this terraqueous globe are the Nantucketer's. For the sea is his; he owns it, as Emperors own em-

pires; other seamen having but a right of way through it. . . .
There lies his home; *there* lies his business, which a Noah's
flood would not interrupt, though it overwhelmed all the millions in China. He lives on the sea as prairie cocks in the
prairie; he hides among the waves, he climbs them as
chamois hunters climb the Alps.

The "hermits, issuing from their ant-hill" give us an image
of the "return" to the world after a "withdrawal." The "blazing banner," the sun—the sun under which the conquerors
and patriarchs, the "naked Nantucketers," divide the oceans
among them. The active forces here are all masculine; the
feminine quantities are acted *upon.* Not far under the surface is a metaphor expressing the primeval scene of capture
and division of the spoils. The whalemen are the rapers of
the world. The "prairie" gives us another image of space, reminding us that the Pacific is an extension of the American
land frontier. "He hides among the waves" we may read "he
withdraws into the trough, the valley"; then, hunting the elusive game, he "climbs the Alps"—that is, he returns.

The style there modulates toward reflection and quiet:

For years he knows not the land; so that when he comes to it
at last, it smells like another world, more strangely than the
moon would to an Earthsman.

In these words there is an abrupt sense of loss, of the need
to turn back. The celestial symbol is now the moon, a feminine symbol. The faculty of sensation now invoked is smell;
the inward, possessive, animal sense now replaces the pro-
jective, aspiring, and conquering one.

And then the introversion, with a reminder that a brutal
power surges under the peaceful surface of meditation as it
does under the delight of the oratorical mood.

With the landless gull, that at sunset folds her wings and is
rocked to sleep between the billows; so at nightfall, the Nantucketer, out of sight of land, furls his sails, and lays him to
his rest, while under his very pillow rush herds of walruses
and whales.

Again the idea of loss: the "land*less* gull." Notice also that the
style is here recapitulating the Fall; two words help to ac-
complish it: "sun*set*" and "night*fall.*" The feeling of a downward motion out of space is invoked, and the sensation of in-
wardness: the folded wings, the furled sails, the female gull
asleep in the trough of the waves. The kinaesthetic sense of
horizontality and relaxation is achieved by "lays him to his
rest"; and the passage leaves us with the idea of femininity,

sleep, and dream; a dream, it may be, of time and the process of nature, the eternal, recapitulant rush of walruses and whales.

Melville's epic style is a rhythm which flows through a life cycle, embodying itself in the appropriate images. At the beginning of the above description of the Nantucketers, we have the style emerging from a context of fact. In the middle of the passage, the style has opened out into the full moon of light and space. The energy, the flight, of the day declines into the myth and fantasy of the afternoon, which in turn modulates into darkness, toward sleep and dream. The first style is a neutral statement of fact. The images of the second style, the mood of oratory, are those we have identified with the return (though they do not all overtly occur in the present passage): Light, Space, Mountain, Tower, Fire, Father, Phallus, Life. The images of the third style, the withdrawal, are: Dark, Time, Valley, Cave, Stone, Son and Mother, Castration, Death. (We might notice here that the sea and the land do not appear as symbolic constants in Melville's books. They have different symbolic meanings in different contexts.)

The Four Levels of Rhetorical Style

Walter E. Bezanson

Walter E. Bezanson discusses four rhetorical techniques Melville uses to create his innovative and compelling prose style. The expository level is straightforward storytelling, the poetic level is featured in key scenes to heighten the moment, the idiomatic level features exaggerated use of language to make a point, and the composite level combines all three previous levels into one smooth but powerful style. Bezanson contends that Melville uses these techniques in a unique combination that explains, in part, the novel's place in literature. Bezanson is a Melville scholar and editor of the Norton edition of Melville's *Israel Potter.*

Of the narrative's several levels of rhetoric [language designed to persuade or impress] the simplest is a relatively straightforward *expository* style characteristic of many passages scattered through the cetological accounts. But it is significant that such passages are rarely sustained, and serve chiefly as transitions between more complex levels of expression. Thus a series of expository sentences in the central paragraph of the chapter on "Cutting In" comes to this point: "This done, a broad, semicircular line is cut round the hole, the hook is inserted, and the main body of the crew striking up a wild chorus, now commence heaving in one dense crowd at the windlass." Whether it cannot or will not, Ishmael's sensibility does not endure for long so bare a diction: "When instantly, the entire ship careens over on her side; every bolt in her starts like the nail-heads of an old house in frosty weather; she trembles, quivers, and nods her frighted mastheads to the sky." The tension is maintained through a following sentence, strict exposition returns in the

Walter E. Bezanson, *"Moby-Dick:* Work of Art," Moby-Dick *Centennial Essays,* edited by Tyrus Hillway and Luther S. Mansfield. Dallas, TX: Southern Methodist University Press, 1953.

next, and the paragraph concludes with an emotionally and grammatically complex sentence which begins with exposition, rises to a powerful image of whale flesh hoisted aloft where "the prodigious blood-dripping mass sways to and fro as if let down from the sky," and concludes with a jest about getting one's ears boxed unless he dodges the swing of the bloody mess. Even in the rhetorically duller chapters of exposition it is a rare paragraph over which heat lightning does not flicker.

THE POETIC LEVEL

A second level of rhetoric, the *poetic*, is well exemplified in Ahab's soliloquy after the great scene on the quarter-deck. As [literary critic F.O.] Matthiessen has shown, such a passage can easily be set as blank verse:

> I leave a white and turbid wake;
> Pale waters, paler cheeks, where'er I sail.
> The envious billows sidelong swell to whelm
> My track; let them; but first I pass.

Because the rhythms here play over an abstract metrical pattern, as in poetry, they are evenly controlled—too evenly perhaps for prose, and the tone seems "literary."

THE IDIOMATIC LEVEL

Quite different in effect is a third level of rhetoric, the *idiomatic* [relating to a group of words established by usage and having meaning not deducible from the individual words, such as "at the drop of a hat"]. Like the poetic it occurs rather rarely in a pure form, but we have an instance in Stubb's rousing exordium [the beginning of a discourse] to his crew:

> "Pull, pull, my fine hearts-alive; pull, my children; pull, my little ones . . . Why don't you break your backbones, my boys? . . . Easy, easy; don't he in a hurry—don't be in a hurry. Why don't you snap your oars, you rascals? Bite something, you dogs! . . ."

Here the beat of oars takes the place of the metronomic meter and allows more freedom. The passage is a kind of rowing song and hence is exceptional; yet it is related in tone and rhythm to numerous pieces of dialogue and sailor talk, especially to the consistently excellent idiom of both Stubb and young Ishmael.

One might venture a fourth level of rhetoric, the *compos-*

ite, simply to assure the inclusion of the narrator's prose at its very best. The composite is a magnificent blending of the expository, the poetic, the idiomatic, and whatever other elements tend to escape these crude categories:

> The Nantucketer, he alone resides and riots on the sea; he alone, in Bible language, goes down to it in ships; to and fro ploughing it as his own special plantation. *There* is his home; *there* lies his business, which a Noah's flood would not interrupt, though it overwhelmed all the millions in China. He lives on the sea, as prairie cocks in the prairie; he hides among the waves, he climbs them as chamois hunters climb the Alps. For years he knows not the land; so that when he comes to it at last, it smells like another world, more strangely than the moon would to an Earthsman. With the landless gull, that at sunset folds her wings and is rocked to sleep between billows; so at nightfall, the Nantucketer, out of sight of land, furls his sails, and lays him to his rest, while under his very pillow rush herds of walruses and whales.

The passage is a great one, blending high and low with a relaxed assurance; after shaking free from the literary constrictions of the opening lines, it comes grandly home. And how does it relate to event and character? Ishmael's memory of the arrival at Nantucket, a mere incident in the movement of the plot, is to Ishmael now an imaginative experience of high order; and this we must know if we are to know about Ishmael. The whole chapter, "Nantucket," is a prose poem in the barbaric jocular vein, and it is as valuable a part of the documentation of Ishmael's experience as are the great "scenes." It is less extraneous to the meaning of the book than are many of the more average passages about Captain Ahab. The same could be said for other great passages of rhetoric, such as the marvelous hymn to spiritual democracy midway in "Knights and Squires." The first level of structure in *Moby-Dick* is the interplay of pressure and control through extraordinarily high rhetorical effects.

Melville's Inventive Use of Language

Newton Arvin

Newton Arvin demonstrates how Melville used language to create a unique atmosphere and energy for *Moby-Dick.* Not only did he use adverbs and adjectives in fresh, unusual ways, he invented new nouns, all in an effort to evoke a sense of movement and energy that would allow the reader to better experience what the crew of the ship was feeling. Newton Arvin was professor of English at Smith College and the author of *Hawthorne* and *Whitman.*

Certainly nothing could be more eloquent of the incandescence out of which *Moby Dick* was written than the . . . extraordinary resourcefulness and inventiveness of Melville's language. For this there is nothing in his earlier books to prepare us fully, though there are hints of it in the best passages of *Redburn* and *White-Jacket.* In general, however, the diction in those books is the current diction of good prose in Melville's time; it has a hardly definable personal quality. Now, in *Moby Dick,* it takes on abruptly an idiosyncrasy of the most unmistakable sort; it is a question now of Melvillean language in the same intense and special sense in which one speaks of Virgilian [referring to first-century B.C. Latin poet Virgil] language, or Shakespearean [referring to seventeenth-century English dramatist William Shakespeare], or Miltonic [referring to seventeenth-century English poet John Milton]. It is a creation, verbally speaking; a great artifice; a particular characterizing idiom; without it the book would not exist. One of its hallmarks, as in all the other cases, is the "signature" furnished by favorite words; the favorite nouns, adjectives, and adverbs that end by coloring the fabric of the book as strongly as the use of a favorite range of hues affects the manner of a painter. Like Virgil, with his *pius, ingens,* and *im-*

manis, or Shakespeare, with his *rich, brave, sweet,* and *gentle,* Melville has his own verbal palette: it is chiefly made up of the words *wild, wildly,* and *wildness, moody* and *moodiness* ("moody Ahab," especially), *mystic* and *mystical, subtle, subtly,* and *subtlety, wondrous* ("most wondrous philosophies"), *nameless, intense,* and *malicious* ("malicious agencies"). One has only to cite these words to suggest how intimately expressive they are of *Moby Dick*'s dark, violent, and enigmatic theme.

MELVILLE INVENTS NEW NOUNS

It is a matter, however, not only of characteristic words, familiar in themselves to readers of Melville's time and ours, but of characteristic *kinds* of words and of words that are again and again his own coinages or at least of a great rarity. One feels, as in all such cases, that the limits of even the English vocabulary have suddenly begun to seem too strict, too penurious [scanty, impoverished], and that the difficult things Melville has to say can be adequately said only by reaching beyond those limits. He does so, perhaps most strikingly, in the constant use he makes of verbal nouns, mostly in the plural, and usually his own inventions; such nouns, for example, as *regardings, allurings, intercedings, wanings, coincidings,* and the nouns one gets in the strangely connotative phrases, "nameless invisible *domineerings*" and "such lovely *leewardings.*" Almost unanalyzable is the effect these have of uniting the dynamism of the verb and the stasis of the substantive. And so of the other abstract nouns Melville loves to use in the plural—*defilements, tranquillities, unfulfilments,* "sorrow's *technicals,*" and "unshored, harborless *immensities.*" In their very unliteral pluralized form these characteristic abstractions become an elusive kind of inverted metaphor. Very different and less metaphorical, but almost as special in their effect, are the nouns Melville habitually constructs with the suffix *-ness* (*localness, landlessness, aborigalness, inter-indebtedness*) or *-ism* (*footmanism, sultanism, Titanism,* and the Carlylean [referring to nineteenth-century Scottish essayist Thomas Carlyle] *vultureism*).

MELVILLE'S CREATIVE USE OF ADJECTIVES AND ADVERBS

Quite as abundant as the unfamiliar nouns are the unfamiliar adjectives and adverbs that do so much to give the style of *Moby Dick* its particular unconformable character. And again, just as verbal nouns are Melville's most characteristic substantives, so adjectives and adverbs based on present or past participles are his most characteristic modifiers; participial adjectives such as *officered, cymballed, omnitooled, unensanguined, uncatastrophied,* "last, *cindered* apple" and "*stumped* and *paupered* arm"; and participial adverbs such as *invokingly, intermixingly, gallopingly, suckingly, postponedly,* and *uninterpenetratingly.* These however are only the most characteristic of his modifiers; a complete list would have to include such rarities as *unsmoothable, familyless, spermy, flavorish, leviathanic,* and *unexempt* (which might have echoed in his mind from *Comus*) or (for adverbs) *diagonically, Spanishly, Venetianly,* and *sultanically.* And even beyond these one would have to glance at the sometimes odd, sometimes magnificent compounds, almost always adjectival, that give so vibrating a life to the pages of the book: "a *valor-ruined* man," "the *message-carrying* air," "the *circus-running* sun," "*teeth-tiered* sharks," and "*god-bullied* hull." There is an energy of verbal inventiveness here that it is hardly too much to call Aeschylean [referring to sixth-century B.C. Greek dramatist Aeschylus] or Shakesperean.

MELVILLE'S CREATION OF VERBAL ENERGY

It does not, curiously, express itself in the formation of unfamiliar verbs so typically as in these other ways; this is a kind of anomaly in a style of which the capacity to evoke movement, action, and all kinds of kinaesthetic [a sense of awareness of the position and movement of the voluntary muscles] sensations is so great. Melville, indeed, uses familiar or not unfamiliar verbs, again and again, with beautiful force; yet the impulsion of some of his finest passages of vehement action depends only partly on these; it depends at least as much on other parts of speech, as a characteristic paragraph such as this will suggest:

> A short rushing sound leaped out of the boat; it was the darted iron of Queequeg. Then all in one welded commotion came an invisible push from astern, while forward the boat seemed striking on a ledge; the sail collapsed and exploded; a gush of scalding vapor shot up near by; something rolled and tumbled like an earthquake beneath us. The whole crew were half suffocated as they were tossed helter-skelter into the white curdling cream of the squall. . . .

Nothing could be finer than a sound leaping out of a boat, or than the "something" that "rolled and tumbled beneath us," but the effect of the passage obviously depends on the vigor with which quite ordinary verbs are used, and at least as much on the vitality of the nouns and adjectives ("welded commotion," "invisible push"). Only rarely, but then sometimes with irresistible effect, does Melville create his own verbs, or virtually create them: "who didst *thunder* him higher than a throne," "he *tasks* me, he *heaps* me," "my fingers . . . began . . . to *serpentine* and *spiralize*," and "skies the most effulgent but *basket* the deadliest thunders." In all these cases, of course, he has boldly made verbs out of nouns or adjectives; and indeed, from this point of view, the manner in which the parts of speech are "intermixingly" assorted in Melville's style—so that the distinction between verbs and nouns, substantives and modifiers, becomes a half unreal one—this is the prime characteristic of his language. No feature of it could express more tellingly the awareness that lies below and behind *Moby Dick*—the awareness that action and condition, movement and stasis, object and idea, are but surface aspects of one underlying reality.

The Four Worlds of Setting

Warner Berthoff

In this excerpt from his book, Warner Berthoff details Melville's use of four settings to represent different aspects of *Moby-Dick*'s theme. To Berthoff, the characters on land are tormented due to lack of freedom, while the sailors who go to sea represent the whaling world of commerce. Berthoff also contends that the setting of the sea represents nature as an indifferent force that cares nothing about humanity or its moral values. These three settings combine to create what Berthoff considers to be Melville's universal setting: a mysterious world of forces that can never fully be known or explained. Professor Berthoff taught literature at Harvard University and is the author of *The Ferment of Realism, 1884–1919*.

Of all Melville's work it was *Moby-Dick* which, in its magnitude and boldness of design, laid the heaviest tribute upon his descriptive powers, and most strenuously tested his ambition to seek out the deeper logic of fact and appearance. It is of course his masterpiece. And one great factor in his accomplishment in *Moby-Dick* is the grandeur and animation of the settings, which in turn do not merely illustrate the book's action and themes but actively create them. The larger part of the narrative is simply the patiently detailed yet consistently high-spirited setting out of a scene sufficiently vast and prodigious to contain the central drama and justify its intensity. Melville's job is to create for us the huge "world" he means dramatically to exploit. This must be done, we are told at the end of Chapter 69, for perfectly practical reasons: a mass of particular facts must be faithfully explained so that when the climax comes we can follow its concentrated moments of action at their proper pace. But what is actually

Warner Berthoff, *The Example of Melville*. Princeton, NJ: Princeton University Press, 1962. Copyright © 1962 by Princeton University Press. Reproduced by permission of the author.

amassed in the long, richly digressive descriptive chronicle spun out by Ishmael is something more than we need for keeping track of the material events of the story. It is its own end and justification. The narrative, in the large, is nothing less than a confession *à fond* [thoroughly] of the several "worlds" human existence marvelously moves through— and in this multiform context Ahab himself is in some danger of becoming only an incidental marvel, one among many, and a rather mechanical one at that. At a certain date in our acquaintance with the book *Moby-Dick* we are no longer in doubt about the outcome; nor can we still be entirely surprised or astounded by the more highly wrought individual passages, of meditation, description, comedy, bravura declamation, analogy-running, or whatever, though we continue to be charmed by them. What does still lay claim on us then, and perhaps more powerfully than ever, is the imaginative coherence and embrace of the whole. . . .

It should be evident that by "setting" I mean something more than the environment or material occasion within which the drama is played out. I mean rather that whole context, as the narrative establishes it, out of which the action rises—a context of idea and feeling as well as of observation and description; I mean all that in the convenient language of recent criticism may be called the "world" of behavior peculiar to an author's vision of existence. In *Moby-Dick* four distinct "worlds" may be defined, and all are fundamental to the import of the novel as Melville built it up.

DRY LAND AS THE WORLD OF DREAM-TORMENTED PEOPLE

(1) With the narrative beginning ashore and staying ashore for twenty-odd chapters, the first "world" put before us is that of the dry land, or at least the thronged edges of it: New York, New Bedford, Nantucket, and the streets, chapels, inns, and offices to be met on the way to the sea. It has its own solid attractions. There are chowder shops and good fellowship, there is the chance of fresh adventure, there is easy access to the earth's far corners and wildest wonders, and there is no shortage of incidental curiosities close at hand. In contrast to the Liverpool of *Redburn* or the New York of *Pierre* and "Bartleby," the cities and harbors of *Moby-Dick* seem hospitable places on the whole, and are presented with a good deal of homely charm and idealizing humor. But the land-world of this part of the book also supplies just as

much motive as is needed for heading us willingly out into the "open independence of the sea." It is, successively, a dream-tormented world of unsatisfied yearnings, a "stepmother" world, a "wolfish" world, a world which "pays dividends" to sharp practice, a finished and unameliorable world of frost, death, teeth-chattering, and the sorrows of the orphaned, and of poverty and hard bargaining; a world finally (as even in the intensifying rush of the book's closing movement the figures of the carpenter and blacksmith do not let us forget) which is continually casting away the human wrecks and derelicts it has stripped and ruined.

PEQUOD AS THE WORLD OF WHALING

(2) It is, in short, the world of men, whose "permanent constitutional condition," we are told, is "sordidness." The next broad context which the narrative begins to build up is also a world of men, but here Melville develops a different emphasis. For this is the self-sufficient world or the quaint, rare, old, noble, trophy-garnished, battle-worn, cannibalistic, melancholy *Pequod*; and Melville's purpose in describing it is to show it as a fit instrument for Ahab and his purpose and for all the "high and mighty business of whaling." The ship takes the center of the stage in Chapter 16, and continues to make a vividly heraldic presence throughout the rest of the book. Primarily a maneuverable slaughterhouse, as the narrative troubles to make spectacularly clear, she is at the same time, in the nature of her business of manufacturing oil, "among the cleanliest things of this tidy earth." Her high qualities are displayed in a series of brilliant and precise physical images: rushing after her boats in the first lowering, beating her way into the sleet and swell of Cape storms, gliding through yellow meadows of brit, pressing up the Sunda Strait in chase of an armada of whales and being chased in turn by armed pirates, and so on. As the concentrated foreground of the book's developing action, she has her own great part to play in it, and a series of descriptive epithets is used, in the manner of epic formulae, to point this up: so we hear of "the tranced ship," the "intense Pequod," "the fated Pequod," "the madly merry and predestinated craft," and—perhaps most beautiful and foreboding of all—"the ivory Pequod."

Coincidentally the ship is shown to be a virtual city of the races and talents of men. From the first we are encouraged to think of her as a paradigm of the marvelous hive of corporate human life (though Melville does not impose that symbolism on the whole novel)—she is at once a parliament, guildhall, factory, and fortress, and goes "ballasted with utilities" like the world-renewing Ark itself. Different phases of the work that goes on aboard her and in her boats furnish metaphors for the different ways of "this world," as in chapters like "The Line" or "Fast Fish and Loose Fish." Mostly, however, the skills and practices of whaling are described for their own sake and in their own full detail, so that the fanciful analogies which are Melville's trademark in chapter-endings are usually erected on an already solid ground of factual interest. Indeed the long succession of passages describing the crew at its jobs makes up a "song for occupations" as comprehensive and ecstatic as Whitman's. Conversely we find Melville turning back to the general routine of common earthly labor for descriptive metaphors, invoking the whole range of its trades, tools, and artifacts in aid of his exposition. Such effects, we must agree, are wonderfully natural in *Moby-Dick*. For merely to describe one feature of the whale's anatomy or of the practical business of stripping it down is to give an impression of surveying no small part of the fantastic material apparatus by which ordinary civilized life is maintained. . . .

In the same vein is this single throwaway sentence in the chapter on the *Pequod's* carpenter: "Like all sea-going ship carpenters, and more especially those belonging to whaling vessels, he was, to a certain off-handed, practical extent, alike experienced in numerous trades and callings collateral to his own; the carpenter's pursuit being the ancient and outbranching trunk of all those numerous handicrafts which more or less have to do with wood as an auxiliary material." I cite it here simply for the way in which, in the casual closing phrases, an altogether incidental piece of information has opened out into something larger and curiously moving—into an acknowledgment of that whole humble order of practical arts which lies at the very root of civilization; arts springing from the support given human life by the simplest commodities of nature, and developed in this case by certain aboriginal chippers and carvers from whom we all must acknowledge descent. Though quite unidealizingly, the sentence serves once more to remind us how *Moby-Dick* is not only a melodrama of the catastrophe of one crazed man's overweening defiance and pride, but an unflaggingly heroic celebration of all mankind's laborious tenure of the physical earth.

No account of the setting of *Moby-Dick* in this common world of human labor and effort would be complete without reference to the accompanying conception, periodically renewed and developed with a great variety of illustration, of "man in the ideal"—which is to say, in the large, in history, in legend, in the depths of his natural being, in all the contributing circumstance of his astonishing character and enterprise. In both the inventoried descriptions of whaling and the bouts of violent action, our attention is constantly drawn back to the men of the *Pequod* and those capacities and virtues we are to know them by. During the long middle stretches of the book, Stubb and Queequeg in particular hold the foreground, observed at this or that office of their trade. They are, in a sense, their trade's representative heroes. Yet the coolness under pressure, the flamboyant nonchalance, the unconscious courage and power to learn to associate with them are simply the practical virtues a fortiori of the whole race of seagoing men. (An early précis of these virtues stands out: the high-flown chapter in praise of those "naked Nantucketers" who "live on the sea, as prairie cocks in the prairie," and have marked out two-thirds of the "terraqueous globe" as their empire.) Melville's democratic idealism and glorification of the "kingly commons" are shown as rooted in fact, in the conduct of ordinary men at their ordinary tasks. But as we gradually learn the force and extent of these virtues, we also gradually get a sense of their limits, and an intimation of other and stranger human attributes less readily described though not a bit less real. On the fringes of the main action hover other, weird, unknown races of men—Lascars, Manillas, Parsees—such as "civilized, domesticated people in the temperate zone only see in their dreams, and that but dimly," races full of the "ghostly aboriginalness of earth's primal generations" and testifying to who knows what further depths in the strange creature, man; and these, too, contribute something to the whole context of the developing narrative.

THE SEA AS THE WORLD OF INDIFFERENT NATURE

(3) The men of the *Pequod* and their exploits are the practical measure also of the next "world" we can discern in

Moby-Dick, the non-human world of the sea and the indifferent elements. At the climax of the first lowering after whales, we get a concentrated image of this confrontation of powers, men against nature. . . . A whale escapes Ishmael's boat; then a squall blows up: "The wind increased to a howl; the waves dashed their bucklers together; the whole squall roared, forked, and crackled around us like a white fire upon the prairie, in which, unconsumed, we were burning; immortal in the jaws of death." Against the exactly realized violence of the scene, this spectacular assertion of heroism does not seem exorbitant. We note, though, that it is an anonymous, corporate heroism. Man alone, acting individually, comes off less well in this awesome setting, or so chapters like "The Mast-Head" and "The Try-Works" powerfully suggest. A different kind of encounter with the "heartless immensity" of the sea drives the cabin-boy Pip out of his mind, adrift among "strange shapes of the unwarped primal world." And though for Ahab, studying his charts and plotting a course, the sea and its mysteries are (at first) only so many instruments for "the more certain accomplishment of that monomaniac thought of his soul," that seems more and more one further proof of madness in him.

For the great expanse of the sea remains, and dwarfs the most extravagant human pretensions; "two thirds of the fair world it yet covers." Its vastness corresponds ambiguously to the grandeur of Ahab's design—corresponds ironically, of course, insofar as it is literally immeasurable, and wholly indifferent to the character and purposes of men. Its very mildness is tormenting; the haunting descriptions of its moments of sun-burnished serenity, prairie-meadow loveliness, or moonlit quietness are invariably shaded by undertones of another sort, so that the stillness is "preternatural," the beauties are "appalling" and "unearthly," "all space" is felt to be "vacating itself of life," and the mild billows support only such a "formless, chance-like apparition of life" as the giant squid. Prolonged exposure to these weird, uncivil spheres of being, in "exile from Christendom and civilization," reduces men (rather, "restores" them, Melville pointedly writes) to a condition of "savagery." And Ishmael apart, the virtues-in-trade of the men of the *Pequod* are chiefly savage virtues. Their splendor is a primitive splendor that suits their character as great warriors, hunters, migratory navigators, efficient agents all of the hive-disciplined assault on nature; we see that they thrive as creatures in a world of creatures, and that none are better adapted to this world than those ghostly aboriginals (Fedallah is one) from "unchanging Asiatic communities" where the "memory of the first man [is] a distinct recollection."

THE MYSTERIOUS AND UNKNOWABLE WORLD

(4) In the nature of their trade's incessant conflict with the non-human elements, the whalemen are also described as peculiarly subject to superstition and legend-making; the book comes naturally by its solid foothold in folklore. This is not just a consequence of the ignorance, the "savagery," of those sailing before the mast. Starbuck, too, is presented as equally superstitious, though by way of "intelligence" rather than "ignorance," and Ishmael himself is distinguished by a fine readiness of sympathy for everything phantomlike and enigmatical. And it is particularly through Ishmael's thoughtful and excited narrative witness that the free passage of our attention is secured into the final, furthest "world" set out in *Moby-Dick*—the world of "inscrutable" things, unknown depths, unanswerable questions, "ungraspable phantoms," "pyramidical silences," hieroglyphic riddles, "celestial thoughts" which are "to reason absurd and frantic," "bodiless" agents, "sourceless primogenitures" and fatherless specters; a world that communicates to men only in signs, portents, and equivocal omens, and seems intelligible only to madmen like Ahab or Pip, yet is felt at times to control human destinies to the last detail.

Inevitably, in evoking this spectral outer sphere of things, certain words, terms, and concepts are used which, though drawn from commonest usage, may reasonably suggest that Melville had some single interpretive scheme for the book as a whole, which it is the job of criticism to identify. Religious allusions are a critical instance of this, and have been a great source of concern to systematizing commentators and exegetes. But when the narrative speaks, in context, of "the interlinked terrors and wonders of God," or relates its heroes' doings to the "mighty, earthly marchings" of the "great democratic God," it does so, I think, without commitment to any identifiable creed or any consistent and paraphrasable "philosophy." Melville's imagination remains, even at these extremities, man-centered and pragmatical. The farthest mysteries of existence remain "those . . . we dream of," and are matched always by the palpable mysteries of human behavior. Consider, for example, the idea of "fate," one of the major terms for the forces conceived to be in play in *Moby-Dick*. By itself, as an independent force, it would be mechanical as a component in the story—and we may well feel that the narrative is least convincing when, in the closing stages, it halfway adopts certain allegoristic conventions of the so-called "fate-tragedy." Only as "fate" is made in one way or another a function of mankind's ordinary and characteristic existence does it take on imaginative validity—when presented, for instance, as a conceit of Ishmael's personal bravado, or, more profoundly, in the haunting evocation of the "weaver-god" (Chapter 102), through the deafening humming of whose ceaseless work the world's "thousand voices" may nevertheless be heard to speak. . . .

The thing that is held to be most horror-striking about the sea and its creatures is the knowledge that they preceded man and will survive him. The whale's terrors are "antemosaic" and "unsourced," and they will exist the same "after all human ages are over"; correspondingly, as the book ends, the indifferent sea rolls on again as it did long before men ever went down to it in ships. . . . For Melville, it is one means among several of expressing perhaps the furthest intuition in *Moby-Dick*, the intuition of an *anima mundi* [a vital force permeating the world], or (to use his words) of a "deep, blue, bottomless soul, pervading mankind and nature," of which the mysterious sea is the prime symbol. All this is most beautifully expressed, I think, in the much remarked chapter in praise of the "mysterious, divine Pacific," as the *Pequod* at last enters its ominous waters—and we may note how the imaginative figure is rendered in terms of the particular souls of individual men:

"There is, one knows not what sweet mystery about this sea, whose gently awful stirrings seem to speak of some hidden soul beneath; like those fabled undulations of the Ephesian sod over the buried Evangelist St. John. And meet it is, that over these sea-pastures, wide-rolling watery prairies and Potters' fields of all four continents, the waves should rise and fall, and ebb and flow unceasingly; for here, millions of mixed shades and shadows, drowned dreams, somnambulisms, reveries; all that we can lives and souls, lie dreaming, dreaming, still; tossing like slumberers in their beds; the ever-rolling waves but made so by their restlessness."

Set against this image, the career of an Ahab cannot make any finally pre-emptive claim on our concern; and we might well say that in such a passage *Moby-Dick* turns away from the design of tragedy even while dramatically the action is preparing to simulate a tragic denouement. The story of Ahab, we feel, does not quite measure up to its own richest imaginative setting.

CHAPTER 2

Symbols and Themes in *Moby-Dick*

Interpretations of *Moby-Dick*

Charles Feidelson Jr.

In this excerpt from Charles Feidelson Jr.'s introduction to *Moby-Dick*, he offers an overview of the major symbols of the novel. He explains how those who live on the land represent an orthodox Christian belief in God, while the sailors who have left the shore represent conflicting moral beliefs, some at odds with the traditional Christian views. Feidelson shows how the quest for the white whale is really Ishmael's quest for a belief system that he can find spiritually fulfilling. Charles Feidelson is the editor and annotator of the Library of Literature edition of *Moby-Dick* and the author of *Symbolism and American Literature*.

Partly because of the diverse influences that came to bear on *Moby Dick*, both from Melville's life and from his reading, it is an extremely complex book that can be regarded in many different ways. Melville himself apparently conceived it in two different forms. His first plan was probably very close to his earlier writings: thinly veiled autobiography used as a vehicle for personal reflection and topical information (in this case about the American whalers). Traces of an original version along these lines remain in the first twenty-two chapters and notably in Chapters I–XV. But as Melville's imagination took hold, he seems to have conceived a more completely fictional work, centering in the story of the White Whale and the quest for him. Probably he revised the opening chapters (I–XXII), as well as large sections that occur later in *Moby Dick*, in the light of his new purpose. The result is a book that swings back and forth from "cetology" to the tale of Ahab and from Melville's own voice to that of an imaginary narrator called Ishmael.

Moby Dick is not necessarily any the worse for this mix-

Charles Feidelson Jr., "Introduction," *Moby-Dick or, The Whale*, by Herman Melville. Indianapolis, IN: The Bobbs-Merrill Company, Inc., 1964. Copyright © 1964 by The Bobbs-Merrill Company, Inc. Reproduced by permission.

ture; indeed, there is every evidence that Melville found both a challenge and an opportunity in welding his two intentions together. But most readers are presumably attracted by the fictional narrative, the excitement and terror of Ahab's voyage. It is a yarn of adventure, a sea tale, but obviously more than that—a fictional action with many of the qualities of epic and romance. Leaving aside all questions of theme and deliberate symbolism, we feel in *Moby Dick* primal patterns of conflict between man and nature, between the glory and the madness of the warrior-hero, between the malevolence and the providential guidance of all that lies beyond man. These motifs are not so much "ideas" as the very substance of the story, inherent in life on the *Pequod*, in the character of Ahab, and in the image of his legendary antagonist. Regarded simply as a narrative, *Moby Dick* is inescapably mythical—full of a primordial vision.

More detailed interpretation depends on which elements of the epic action are singled out for emphasis and how they are combined to formulate a theme. If we begin with the natural world—the nonhuman environment that bulks so large in the book—we may see it as merely indifferent to men, who read human moral values into it. Or we may see it as an eternal mystery, incomprehensible to men but ordered by God. Or we may view it through Ahab's eyes, as primarily evil *because* it is incomprehensible, whether or not it is ruled by God. Or we may side with Ishmael, the pantheist, who wants to identify nature with divinity. Or we may combine the visions of Ahab and Ishmael, as Ishmael is always forced to do, into an ambiguous union of natural good and evil, divinity and neutrality, meaning and nothingness.

PEOPLE ON SHORE SPEAK FOR GOD

The sense of nature as a benign mystery, God's world, belongs to the spokesmen of the "shore," the normal nineteenth-century American civilization from which the *Pequod* sets out. Father Mapple before the sailing and the first mate, Starbuck, on the ship are the exponents of religious and social normality. They urge a humility, an acquiescence both in the gifts and in the prohibitions of God, without which the civilization of the land could not exist. These two characters are often regarded as the key to *Moby Dick*, which thereby becomes a fundamentally Christian book. The entire voyage of Ahab can be interpreted as a blasphemous departure from the "land" values that ought to rule it even on the ocean. In this sense, Ahab is damned because he diverts his great gifts from their proper role—the service of God through the practical service of his fellow men. He is doubly damned because he knows his duty and willfully flouts it. And he destroys all who follow him, both those who fall victim to his teachings and those, like Starbuck, who demur but are too weak to defy him.

SAILORS REPRESENT CONFLICTING MORAL BELIEFS

Yet there are radical differences between the ocean-world and the land-world in *Moby Dick.* One difference is made clear both by Melville's characterization of the other mates, Stubb and Flask, and by his treatment of the crew. Though Stubb and Flask are not actively hostile to Starbuck's Christian values, they have little need for his or any other ultimate meanings. The whale they fiercely pursue is morally neutral, like themselves. The crew, on the other hand, and especially Daggoo and Tashtego, the towering harpooneers, are positively anti-Christian. In these savages, the amoral activity of Stubb and Flask becomes a positive moral principle of ferocity, which has its correlative in the deliberate ferocity of Moby Dick. In Fedallah, Ahab's harpooneer, ferocity verges over into a melancholy devil worship, with the White Whale in the role of supernatural evil. But even Ishmael's pagan friend Queequeg, who is neither especially ferocious nor a devil worshiper, is wholly at odds with any "civilized" values. All these men of the ocean are governed in one way or another by the unconscious, irrational mind, in contrast to the rational consciousness that formulates the religion and laws of Christian civilization. It may be a benign unconsciousness in Queequeg, a violent and destructive compulsion in the other crewmen, and a mere unreflective energy in Stubb and Flask; but in all cases it suggests a kind of man whose qualities, for good or ill, lie outside the categories proper to the land. Thus the little Negro Pip, who at first clearly belongs among the landsmen, takes on some of the qualities of the ocean-man in his madness after he has been cast into the sea.

Our attitude toward Ahab and Ishmael and the White Whale largely depends on whether or not we accept the notion of a distinctive ocean-world with problems and values of its own. If we take Father Mapple and Starbuck as Melville's spokesmen, then Ahab, as already mentioned, is a Satanic figure, too proud to share in the human condition; the men of the sea are evil insofar as they side with him, and good insofar as they can be adapted to civilized purposes, like Stubb and Flask, or at least have a human sociability, like Queequeg and Pip. But the fact is that Ahab in all his madness commands our respectful attention; he seems to be in touch with realities that civilized life covers up and evades. He himself may be (indeed, has been) viewed as Melville's spokesman, in which case *Moby Dick* is a frontal attack on God, and the ocean-world is a place where defiant hatred can finally be shouted rather than whispered. A less extreme interpretation would see him neither as a Satanic egoist nor as a heroic antagonist of God, but as a "tragic" hero (Melville's own term). The ocean, then, would be the world as *given* to him, not a world he arbitrarily imagines— a revelation of tragic incongruities in God, nature, and man. Ahab, from this point of view, is not rejecting the human condition but suffering it and striving to comprehend it. If he is arrogant, his undertaking and his agony are enormous; if he cannot achieve any final faith or peace, as the tragic hero has traditionally managed to do, it is because he has been cast into a universe beyond the traditional tragic scene—a universe without any certainties whatsoever.

THE AMBIGUITY OF ISHMAEL'S CHARACTER

The sailor Ishmael is plainly no villain. But it is harder to say whether he is a hero and, if so, what sort of hero he may be. He shows only a mild interest in the religion of Father Mapple. Initially, at least, he does not aspire to be a servant of the Christian God but wants to become part of a pantheistic world spirit, which he consistently associates with the ocean as opposed to the land. He has no stake in civilization but finds a private community outside society in his friendship with the uncivilized Queequeg. Yet he learns that these propensities are perilous: The other side of pantheism and Queequeg is diabolism and Fedallah; the other side of the heavenly voyage is the ferocious whale hunt and the agony of Ahab. The question in Ishmael's case is: What saves him? Does the Christian Providence, moved either by Ishmael's basic humility or by its own mysterious choice, intervene to snatch him from death? Or does his survival symbolize the victory of his own pantheistic faith in life, triumphing over the terrors that also inhabit the sea?

THE MEANINGS OF THE WHALE

All these and various other possibilities of interpretation are in question when we ask what Melville meant by the White Whale. That issue cannot be raised in isolation, as it often is. The meaning of Moby Dick is bound up with the meaning we find in the entire book to which he gives his name. We may identify him with the blank indifference of nature; with the leviathan that God sent to chastise Jonah; with the "unconscious understandings" of the crew; with the Devil-God who rules Ahab's world; or with the World Spirit of Ishmael. Probably none of these is an adequate reading in itself, but certainly no interpretation is adequate that fails to take into account the multiplicity of possible meanings in the White Whale and in *Moby Dick* as a whole. Like the story it tells, our reading of this book is a kind of quest. The point at which we emerge, the conclusion we reach, is largely determined by the point at which we enter, the assumption from which we start. But between these points we can try to see as much as possible and then return to make the journey along another path.

Sharks as a Symbol of Human Nature

Robert Zoellner

Robert Zoellner demonstrates how Melville uses sharks throughout the novel to symbolize the darker side of human nature. For example, the image in the novel of thousands of sharks ripping chunks out of a whale is used to imply that humans can act just as greedily and without regard for others. However, Zoellner argues that Melville sees greed as not just something to be crushed, but a fundamental part of being human that reflects a sharkish universe in general. Therefore, we must become "well-governed sharks," by acknowledging the strength for survival that our sharkness gives us, but tempering sharkish impulses with our desire for fulfillment beyond mere survival. Robert Zoellner is an English professor at Colorado State University.

The full meaning of this frightful sharkishness . . . does not come clear, however, until almost halfway through *Moby-Dick* when Fleece, the *Pequod's* black cook, delivers his homily to the sharks. This second sermon, in many respects contrapuntal to Father Mapple's sermon on Jonah, establishes the philosophical and moral parameters requisite for a true understanding. . . . When, at midnight, Stubb's whale-steak supper is disturbed by the mastications of thousands upon thousands of sharks swarming about the dead whale lashed to the ship's side, the petulant second mate orders old Fleece to "preach to 'em!" in the hope that decorum will be restored. Opening on an appropriately pastoral note, Fleece addresses the sharks as "Belubed fellow-critters":

> Dough you is all sharks, and by natur wery woracious, yet I zay to you, fellow-critters, dat dat woraciousness—'top dat dam slappin' ob de tail! How you tink to hear, 'spose you keep up such a dam slappin' and bitin' dare? [Here a profane re-

monstrance from Stubb on profanity, and then the sermon continues.] Your woraciousness, fellow-critters, I don't blame ye so much for; dat is natur, and can't be helped; but to gobern dat wicked natur, dat is de pint. You is sharks, sartin; but if you gobern de shark in you, why den you be angel; for all angel is not'ing more dan de shark well goberned. Now, look here, bred'ren, just try wonst to be cibil, a helping yourselbs from dat whale. Don't be tearin' de blubber out your neighbour's mout, I say. Is not one shark dood right as toder to dat whale? And, by Gor, none on you has de right to dat whale; dat whale belong to some one else. I know some o' you has berry brig mout, brigger dan oders; but den de brig mouts sometimes has de small bellies; so dat the brigness ob de mout is not to swallar wid, but to bite off de blubber for de small fry ob sharks, dat can't get into de scrouge to help demselves.

Over a century after Melville wrote these lines, one can only feel embarrassment at such evidence—pervasive in nineteenth-century American literature from [nineteenth-century American novelist James] Fenimore Cooper on—that possession of moral sensitivity and high creative gifts does not necessarily arm one against the prejudices and stereotypical thinking of one's culture. Melville's conception of the black personality in *Moby-Dick*—and most especially in Pip and Fleece—must be a source of chagrin to all twentieth-century readers. But revulsion at this tasteless attempt to draw on the crude traditions of "darky" humor should not prevent us from seeing that Melville is being crude with a purpose. For the fact is that the black pseudo-dialect of Fleece's sermon is a deliberate mask. All one has to do is rewrite the sermon in "straight" English to see that we are in actuality dealing with someone other than a sleepy ship's cook.

The tip-off is the word *voracious*, masked as *woracious*. Every other character in *Moby-Dick* speaks according to his station and background. Ahab has been to college as well as among the cannibals; Ishmael is a bookish ex-schoolmaster; Starbuck is deeply read in the Bible—and all three speak in a manner commensurate with these facts. Stubb and Flask speak the rough-and-ready idiom one expects from subordinate ship's officers. Queequeg, Tashtego, and Daggoo likewise express themselves in locutions reflecting their wild vitality. But this correlation breaks down with Fleece. Not only does the old man employ bookish adjectives such as *voracious* and *civil*, and learned verbs such as *to govern*. He also manages, in the compass of some twenty lines, to touch upon the issues of the *nature of life,* the place of *government,* the need for *civility,* the question of *inherent rights,* the sanctity of *private property,* the demands of *charity,* the problem of *equality,* the source and nature of *good and evil,* and the moral relationship of the *strong to the weak.* This is an astonishing midnight performance for a half-awake cook on a lowly American whaler. Fleece, it seems clear, is mouthing somebody else's words. It is equally clear that the "somebody else" is Melville himself. The old cook's sermon is perhaps the only place in *Moby-Dick* where, for a certainty, the mind of Melville himself can be detected moving beneath the dense web of the textual surface. Fleece's synthetic dialect represents a not-very-successful attempt to construct a verbal screen of maximum opacity, a diversionary mask to hide the sudden and unprecedented presence of the author in the fictional world he has created. Such an analysis prevents us from dismissing Fleece, as [literary critic] Warner Berthoff does, as a mere "figure of fun." Fleece represents instead a unique instance of auctorial intrusion into an otherwise hermetic fictional world. As such, his sermon demands that close attention reserved for unique literary events.

SHARKS CAN BE BOTH DEVILS AND ANGELS

The importance of what Fleece has to say lies in the differing reactions which Ishmael and the *Pequod's* cook exhibit when confronted with the fact of sharkishness. When Ishmael gazes over the side at the thousands of sharks insensately tearing head-sized chunks of blubber out of Stubb's whale, he speaks despairingly of *devils.* When, less than a page later, Fleece lowers a lantern and contemplates the same scene, he speaks of *angels.* This shift from devil to angel schematizes a major resolution in *Moby-Dick.* But the precise nature of that resolution cannot be established until another and quite distinct level of meaning is disentangled from Fleece's rambling monologue. This is the level on which Fleece's sermon can be read as a commentary on Father Mapple's. Jonah's story is a tale of "the sin, hardheartedness, suddenly awakened fears, the swift punishment, repentance, prayers, and finally the deliverance and joy of Jonah." The prophet's sin is "wilful disobedience of the command of God." "And if we obey God," Father Mapple asserts, "we must disobey ourselves; and it is in this disobeying ourselves, wherein the hardness of obeying God consists."

Self-disobedience, then, is the norm of Father Mapple's
Christian universe. Jonah is not persuaded to do God's bidding. Rather, he is forced to—forced, that is, to disobey himself. Overwhelmed by the "hard hand of God," he becomes
"aghast Jonah," reduced to "cringing attitudes." As with
Jonah, so with the ship's crew. When they pity him, refusing
to cast him overboard, "seek[ing] by other means to save the
ship," God simply increases the intensity of the storm until
the crew disobey their charitable instincts and throw Jonah
over the side. Father Mapple's version of the Christian message demands, in short, that we go against our own natures
and deny our own humanity. It is Augustinian [referring to
fifth-century Christian theologian Saint Augustine] and
Calvinist [referring to sixteenth-century Scottish Christian
reformer John Calvin] Christianity, that same Stylitic [Chris-
tian ascetics] tradition which, over the centuries, has persuaded some men to suppress their sexuality, some to abort
their natural talents, others to withdraw into monastic isolation, and still others to flagellate their living flesh.

Put in these terms—man's relationship to his own human
nature—the connection between Father Mapple's sermon
and Fleece's sermon becomes immediately apparent. Fleece
deals explicitly with the *nature* of the living, responding
creature. He begins by reminding the blood-lusting rabble
over the *Pequod's* side that "you is all sharks, and by natur
wery woracious." Interrupted by Stubb, he resumes by making the same point again. "Your woraciousness, fellow-
critters, I don't blame ye so much for; dat is natur, and can't
be helped." Having twice asserted the intractability of
"natur," Fleece then proves his thesis by urging the principal
imperatives of Christian civilization upon his congregation.
They should, for example, try to be civil, learning to love one
another: "Now, look here, bred'ren, just try wonst to be cibil.
. . . Don't be tearin' de blubber out your neighbour's mout, I
say." He urges them to be sensitive to each other's rights: "Is
not one shark dood right as toder [as good a right as another]
to dat whale?" The sharks should also recognize the prior
rights of possession and private ownership: "And, by Gor,
none on you has de right to dat whale; dat whale belong to
someone else." Above all, Fleece pleads for charity and the
golden rule, especially as these apply to the strong and the
gifted: "I know some o' you has berry brig mout, brigger dan
oders; . . . de brigness ob de mout is not to swallar wid, but

to bite off de blubber for de small fry ob sharks." In short, in an unmistakable parody of Father Mapple's view of man, Fleece asks the sharks to "disobey themselves," to go against their own sharkish natures. He asks them to suppress, or more precisely, *extirpate* their own sharkishness. He asks them to *stop being sharks.* Lest we miss the point, Stubb makes it explicit. "Well done, old Fleece!" he exclaims, "that's Christianity." But Fleece's homily is, on this level, an exercise in futility:

> No use goin' on; de dam willains will keep a scrougin' and slappin' each oder, Massa Stubb; dey don't hear one word; no use apreachin' to such dam g'uttons as you call 'em, till dare bellies is full, and dare bellies is bottomless; and when dey do get 'em full, dey wont hear you den; for den dey sink in de sea, go fast to sleep on de coral, and can't hear not'ing at all, no more, for eber and eber.

The meaning is clear: it is utterly hopeless to urge sharks to stop being sharks—or men to stop being men. Moral and ethical imperatives which demand the suppression, the distortion, or (most especially) the *extirpation* of essential nature can lead only to alienation from self and hypocrisy toward others.

HUMANS MUST BECOME WELL-GOVERNED SHARKS

But Fleece delivers his sermon not only to the finny and aqueous sharks over the *Pequod's* side. Standing at his shoulder to hear the exhortation is Stubb, a human shark who likes his steak blood-rare, but who in this respect is no different from Queequeg and Peleg and Bildad and Ahab, and indeed the entire crew of the *Pequod*—all of them, as Starbuck has it, "Whelped somewhere by the sharkish sea." What Fleece has to say applies even to ex-schoolmaster Ishmael, who despite his bookish mildness, admits that "I myself am a savage, owning no allegiance but to the King of the Cannibals; and ready at any moment to rebel against him." For these bipedal and terrestrial sharks, Fleece introduces the idea of control, of *government.* This level of the sermon is signaled by the old man's addressing his congregation as "Belubed fellow-critters," and, a little later, as "bred'ren." Fleece speaks thus to Brother Shark because he knows that Stubb, and all of us, share with these most insensately vicious monsters of the deep a hankering taste for the carnivorous and the ensanguined. The whole sermon is on this level deeply ironic, darkly tinged with an inverted and demonic Franciscanism [referring to Christian order founded in 1209 by St. Francis of Assisi]. For the oceanic sharks any degree of self-government is obviously out of the question. The failure of the sermon to produce the quiet and decorum which Stubb demands is proof enough of that. But Fleece's *human* "fellow-critters" are another matter. "Your woraciousness, fellow-critters, . . . is natur, and can't be helped; but to gobern dat wicked natur, dat is de pint. You is sharks, sartin; but if you gobern de shark in you, why den you be angel; for all angel is not'ing more dan de shark well goberned."

Nothing could be more startling than this abrupt introduction of the idea of the *angelic* into Fleece's dark expostulation. Contemplating the same bloody scene only a page earlier, Ishmael spoke, not of the angelic, but of the demonic. "If you have never seen [this] sight," he despairingly admonished us, "then suspend your decision about the propriety of devil-worship, and the expediency of concilating the devil." The contrast is too sharp to be accidental; Melville, once again, is after a meaning. The key to that meaning lies in the differing responses which Ishmael and Fleece bring to the idea of essential and intractable nature. Ishmael, at this point in *Moby-Dick*, is intellectually and emotionally incapable of accepting the fact that sharks are sharks. Evidently, nothing less than the absolute extirpation of the sharks' very nature would satisfy him. His residual Christianity makes him feel that only by ceasing to be sharks, only by disobeying themselves, could the sharks transcend the "diabolism" which he sees them as representing. Since such a solution is impossible, Ishmael despairs, preparing to acknowledge the malign and bow to the demonic in life.

Fleece, in sharp contrast, imperturbably accepts essential nature. Voraciousness, in sharks and in humans, "is natur, and can't be helped." Then, in a crucial turn of thought, Fleece postulates the idea, not of self-disobedience, not of extirpation, but of *government*: ". . . but to gobern dat wicked natur, dat is de pint." The old man makes it clear that "government" is not the source of good, but rather only the *means* by which good is brought into being. In contrast to the radical dualism implicit in Ishmael's response to the feasting sharks, Fleece reveals himself as a monist, asserting that good and evil do *not* spring from distinct sources or from discrete vitalities, but rather from the same source and the same vitality. "You is sharks, sartin," he tells his congregation; "but if you gobern de shark in you, why den you be angel; *for all angel is not'ing more dan de shark well goberned*" (italics mine). It is, to say the least, disconcerting to conceive of the angelic choirs as consisting of rank upon rank of seraphic predators and cherubic carnivores. It is even more disconcerting to conceive of the God of Hosts as a Benign Shark, a Deific Cannibal. But this is precisely what old Fleece means. He is postulating sharkishness, the ineluctably rapacious life-dynamism of the self-sustaining individual, as the bedrock of animate creation, the raw stuff from which moral vitality—either Ahabian or Ishmaelian—must be made if it is to be made at all. He is saying that *both* good and evil spring from one source: sharkishness. He is explicitly rejecting Father Mapple's Christian idea of extirpation—the obsessive and foredoomed effort to eliminate absolutely the vicious, the nasty, or the simply unpleasant aspects of essential nature. Fleece knows that the extirpation of sharkishness would be the extirpation of good. Just as, to Ishmael, Queequeg is "George Washington cannibalistically developed," so the angel is the shark morally developed. The good man is simply the good shark. This is the burden of Fleece's sermon.

The Characters' Conflicting Perceptions of Moby Dick

R.E. Watters

R.E. Watters discusses how each of the main characters in the novel has a different perception of Moby Dick, and that their perceptions reveal their true natures. More important, the fact that each of these characters cannot change their perceptions to see the whale as meaning more than one thing contributes to their destruction. Only Ishmael learns to see the whale, and therefore the world itself, as more complex than a projection of one's self. Watters is a noted literature scholar and author of *Check List of Canadian Literature and Background Materials, 1628–1950.*

"To produce a mighty book," wrote Herman Melville, "you must choose a mighty theme. No great and enduring volume can ever be written on the flea, though many there be who have tried it." Everybody will now grant that *Moby Dick* is a mighty book on a mighty theme—even though there is little agreement about the definition of that theme.

At the core of the problem is the interpretation of the white whale himself. Every reader capable of seeing more in the book than an exciting adventure story or a treatise on an extinct maritime industry soon becomes an enthusiastic fisherman, endeavouring "to hook the nose of this leviathan.". . .

Nevertheless, the very disagreement of the critics may indicate something of value. Perhaps we might take a hint from Ahab and dive to "a little lower layer" for the universal principle which may be putting "forth the mouldings of its features" through the different white whales. Might it not have been Melville's own intention to invest his great symbolic leviathan with a plurality of meanings?

R.E. Watters, "The Meanings of the White Whale," *Discussions of* Moby-Dick, edited by Milton R. Stern. Boston: D.C. Heath and Company, 1960.

Simultaneously with his posing the problem, Melville created a formidable body of conflicting interpretations. The whalers on board the *Pequod* and the other whaling ships differed about the meaning of the white whale. At least, they differed when they were not hypnotized by Ahab's "evil magic," as Ishmael calls it, into accepting Ahab's interpretation that the whale was "in some dim, unsuspected way . . . the gliding great demon of the seas of life." Many readers are similarly hypnotized into accepting one or more of Ahab's views; Ahab, be it noted, had more than one. . . .

There is a clear hint in the very chapter of *Moby Dick*, where Melville, discussing the fascination exercised on men by water, says: "Surely all this is not without meaning. And still deeper the meaning of that story of Narcissus [a myth about a Greek youth who fell in love with his reflection in the water], who because he could not grasp the tormenting, mild image he saw in the fountain, plunged into it and was drowned. But that same image, we ourselves see in all rivers and oceans. It is the image of the ungraspable phantom of life, and this is the key to it all." The same idea is developed much more explicitly, however, in the wonderful chapter on the doubloon. The gold coin which is nailed to the mast to reward the man who first sights the white whale is, as the Negro Pip calls it, "the ship's navel." One morning, late in the cruise, all the leading characters of the book contemplate this navel, so to speak—and discover themselves. As Ahab recognized, "this round gold is but the image of the rounder globe, which, like a magician's glass, to each and every man in turn but mirrors back his own mysterious self." Here is the Narcissus idea again. And after Ahab, Starbuck, Stubb, Flask, and the others have all read themselves in reading the coin, the little Negro, whose "insanity is heaven's sense," thrice repeats his cryptic comment: "I look, you look, he looks; we look, ye look, they look." As William Ellery Sedgwick has pointed out in *Herman Melville: The Tragedy of Mind*, what Pip is saying, in effect, is that although the object (the coin) remains the same, and the process or verb ("look") remains the same, yet the one change in the subject of the verb makes the whole meaning different.

So the meaning of the coin—and the meaning of the white whale—depends on the subject, on the one who does the looking. There are therefore innumerable meanings for the white whale. . . .

COMMON PEOPLE VIEW THE WHALE AS THREATENING

Very early in the book Melville says that not all whalemen even "knew of [the white whale's] existence; only a few of them, comparatively, had knowingly seen him; while the number who as yet had actually and knowingly given battle to him, was small indeed." Most whalemen—the common people—had at best heard rumours and shared some general beliefs about this unseen and unknown whale: that he was immense, ferocious, malignant, and not without apparent intelligence. Such ordinary men, like their fellows aboard the *Pequod*, looked upon the white whale as dangerous and intelligent, and therefore perhaps "evil" in the sense of harmful—just as they would no doubt regard a vicious dog as a malignant creature. But such an attitude did not make them take up any quarrel with the creator or with the universe. They thought of the white whale as a particular danger, not as the deity or an agent of the deity, not as the devil or an agent of the devil, and not as a symbol of the inherent evil or unintelligibility of the universe. A few of the "superstitiously inclined," as Ishmael calls them, go a little further and conceive of the white whale as immortal and ubiquitous—but even that advance leaves them far removed from the interpretations of either Ahab or Ishmael.

STARBUCK VIEWS THE WHALE AS A "DUMB BRUTE"

These ordinary men were, in their interpretations, far closer to Starbuck, whose orthodox piety was shocked at Ahab's seeking "vengeance on a dumb brute . . . that simply smote thee from blindest instinct!" Before this voyage, Starbuck had only "heard" of the white whale, and to him that whale always remained a "dumb brute," a natural even if concentrated manifestation of normal life in the universe of whaling, part of the danger and death one risked in "the business we follow." Such perils, which had been fatal to both his father and his brother, were no doubt "evil" in one sense, but at worst were only the tragic accompaniments to a hazardous profession. He killed whales for a living, not for adventure, let alone any "heaven-insulting purpose." He is a "staid, steadfast man" who is best pleased when "duty and profit" go "hand in hand." His attitude towards the white whale is simply that the risk is too great for the profit that might accrue. He is unconcerned with any possible glory, for he is no "crusader after perils." He is piously and sincerely content to trust in God to run the universe while he does his duty to the owners and hunts whales for his living. He dies performing his duty and praying to his God.

STUBB VIEWS THE WHALE AS A CHALLENGE

To Stubb, the casual, happy-go-lucky second mate, whaling is simply glorious fun. "Think not" is his "eleventh commandment" and "a laugh's the wisest, easiest answer to all that's queer." Like Starbuck, he leaves the running of the universe to other hands; but whereas Starbuck trusts in a personal God, Stubb is a fatalist: he finds "unfailing comfort" in his belief that "it's all predestinated." Ahab has a similar fatalism—but, gifted with high intellectual powers, Ahab finds no comfort in it. Stubb willingly follows his captain who, he says, acts on the right principle: "live in the game, and die in it!" Nevertheless, Ahab has little respect for jolly Stubb, whereas he has some for Starbuck who is capable of understanding Ahab's purposes and motives, while disapproving them. "Down, dog, and kennel!" Ahab once snarls at Stubb; and later, when Stubb laughs at the wreck of Ahab's boat and calls it "the thistle the ass refused," Ahab calls him "a soulless thing . . . Did I not know thee brave as fearless fire (and as mechanical) I could swear thou wert a poltroon." By whale-oil light Stubb eats whale-steak as a delight to his palate, just as he hunts whales for the thrill, the joyous adventure. He impiously prays to the corpusants, damns the devil out of bravado, and blasphemously scoffs at God. In short, he is almost completely devoid of a sense of values, completely indifferent to spiritual and intellectual affairs. Life to him is a jolly game, a high-spirited frolic. His attitude towards the white whale is clearly that it is to be merely the crowning adventure, a daring challenge—nothing more. Even death becomes but an occasion for witticisms.

In Starbuck and Stubb, therefore, we have representatives of two large groups of readers: those who prefer to regard the white whale as merely a dangerous specimen of sea life, without philosophical or symbolic connotations; and those who give no thought to the matter at all provided the adventure be exciting. As Ahab says, "Starbuck is Stubb reversed, and Stubb is Starbuck; and ye two are all mankind."

In Flask we have a slightly different point of view or interpretation. He is described as pugnacious, destructive, indifferent or cruel (he stamps carelessly on Daggoo's shoulders while perching there for better lookout, and he probes the ulcerous growth on the sick whale). He is the complete materialist, "so utterly lost . . . to all sense of reverence for the many marvels . . . and mystic ways [of whales] . . . that in his poor opinion, the wondrous whale was but a species of magnified mouse, or at least water-rat, requiring only a little circumvention and some small application of time and trouble in order to kill and boil. . . . He followed these fish for the fun of it." If Starbuck is the careful man in the whale fishery, and Stubb the adventurer, then Flask is the ignorant and destructive mediocrity. All he sees in the gold doubloon is a certain number of cigars, and the white whale himself presumably is only worth so many more. In the face of death from Moby Dick his last thought is of money. . . .

FEDALLAH VIEWS THE WHALE AS AN INSTRUMENT OF FATE

Fedallah's point of view or interpretation is also enigmatic. He has, of course, a mysterious affinity, sometimes a kind of identity, with Ahab, though they rarely speak to each other, and though Ahab "shunned Fedallah" when he was choosing a man to hoist him aloft to a lookout point. Fedallah compares the wrinkles on the right whale's head to the lines in his hand, in a not dissimilar gesture to Queequeg's comparing his tattooing to the signs on the doubloon. Fedallah merely "makes a sign" to the doubloon and "bows himself" in a way which makes Stubb label him a "fire worshipper." On the night of the corpusants, Fedallah kneels "beneath the doubloon and the flame" and is used as a footstool by Ahab in his harangue to the "clear spirit of the fire." Fedallah is a fatalist, who foresees his own doom and that of Ahab, yet chooses to let Ahab misinterpret his prophetic messages. To Fedallah, the white whale means death and a horrible "hearse"—an instrument of a foreseen fate, just as Fedallah himself is an instrument of Ahab's all-consuming purpose. But the problem of which is the agent and which the principal here (as elsewhere) becomes involved, for to make Fedallah's fate come to pass Ahab and his quest are as "instrumental" as Moby Dick himself. For Fedallah, the meanings of the white whale and of Ahab coincide.

AHAB VIEWS THE WHALE AS A MALIGNANT DIVINITY

Ahab's complex conception of the white whale has received by far the most attention. It is not therefore necessary to discuss it here at any length. To Ahab, Moby Dick was a composite entity—physical power, wilful intelligence, and malignant divinity—a trinity of body, mind, and spirit in opposition to Ahab. Which of the three a reader chooses to emphasize as *the* meaning for Ahab is, as Melville clearly implies, a reflection of the reader's own personal character.

From his first encounter with Moby Dick, Ahab has hated him, and "at last came to identify with him, not only all his bodily woes, but all his intellectual and spiritual exasperations. . . . All that most maddens and torments; all that stirs up the lees of things; all truth with malice in it; all that cracks the sinews and cakes the brain; all the subtle demonisms of life and thought; all evil, to crazy Ahab, were visibly personified, and made practically assailable in Moby Dick. He piled upon the whale's white hump the sum of all the general rage and hate felt by his whole race from Adam down. . . ." Ahab is not sure whether the white whale is "agent" or "principal"; it is enough for him that the whale should be assailable. The whale may be only a "pasteboard mask," like "all visible objects," but in him Ahab sees "outrageous strength, with an inscrutable malice sinewing it," and he hates that "inscrutable thing." As he says on the third day of the chase, "all the things that most exasperate and outrage mortal man, all these things are bodiless, but only bodiless as objects, not as agents. There's a most special, a most cunning, oh, a most malicious difference!" Ahab's "great natural intellect" had itself become an agent, the "living instrument" of his monomania, which made him intent, not on profitable cruises or dutiful responsibility to his crew, not even on glory and adventure, but "on an audacious, immitigable, and supernatural revenge," impious defiance, and despotic self-gratification.

ISHMAEL VIEWS THE WHALE AS THE INDEFINITE UNIVERSE

Whereas Ahab's interpretations of the white whale have received much attention, Ishmael's have been almost equally neglected. But before Ahab reveals his problem and his purpose of hunting the white whale, Ishmael has already told us that "the problem of the universe" was revolving in him. When Ahab binds the crew with an oath to hunt Moby Dick to his death, the occasion produced in Ishmael "a wild, mystical, sympathetical feeling"; as he says, "Ahab's quenchless feud seemed mine." He gave himself "up to the abandonment of the time and the place; but while yet all a-rush to encounter the whale, could see naught in that brute but the deadliest ill."

Ishmael, however, is a thoughtful man—a Melville. And the problem of the universe and/or the whale went on revolving in him. He devotes an entire chapter to the attempt to say "what the white whale . . . at times . . . was to me." He begins with these words: "Aside from those more obvious considerations touching Moby Dick, which could not but occasionally awaken in any man's soul some alarm, there was another thought, or rather vague, nameless horror concerning him, which at times by its intensity completely overpowered all the rest; and yet so mystical and well nigh ineffable was it, that I almost despair of putting it in a comprehensible form. It was the whiteness of the whale that above all things appalled me. But how can I hope to explain myself here; and yet, in some dim, random way, *explain myself I must, else all these chapters might be naught*" (my italics). The rest of this famous chapter on the whiteness of the whale discusses *this* meaning—and it is surely significant that *no one else, not even Ahab,* appears to be troubled by this aspect of Moby Dick. To Ahab and the others the whiteness is merely a useful but fortuitous aid in identifying a particular whale; only to Ishmael has the whiteness any further meaning at all.

Ishmael recognizes that there are innumerable "sweet, and honourable, and sublime" associations with whiteness, that, indeed, "whiteness . . . is at once the most meaning symbol of spiritual things, nay, the very veil of the Christian's Deity; and yet . . . it is the intensifying agent in things the most appalling to mankind." The root of the horror inspired in him by whiteness, Ishmael concludes, seems to be that whiteness symbolizes the "indefiniteness," the "heartless voids and immensities," the "dumb blankness" of the universe. Later, on reading about the "most wondrous phenomenon which the secret seas have hitherto revealed to mankind," the great squid, which appeared as a silent "great white mass . . . like a snow slide . . . no perceptible face or front . . . no conceivable token of either sensation or instinct; but . . . an unearthly, formless, chancelike apparition of life," we are reminded of these phrases in Ishmael's conclusion. But in the chapter on "The Whiteness of the Whale" Ishmael goes on to interpret the whiteness as a symbol that the universe is a formless, indefinite blank, and that beauty and meaning are "but subtile deceits, not actually inherent in substances, but only laid on from without" by the observer. Here we quite obviously have again the idea of "I look, you look, he looks. . . ." The universe, this "rounder globe" is like the doubloon, and both are like the white whale—a blank existence upon which form or meaning is projected by the observer. Ishmael goes farther, to consider that light itself "remains white or colourless in itself" and requires a "medium" (presumably the "eyes" of some observer) if any colour is to be seen by the light. Even Ahab himself, when his "tormented spirit" was for a time dissociated from his monomaniac purpose, becomes a meaningless being. Melville employs the same metaphor of light to express this point, in the chapter entitled "The Chart," which explains how sometimes there would be a spontaneous rebellion of Ahab's "living principle or soul" against "the characterizing mind, which at other times employed it for its outer vehicle or agent. . . . Therefore, the tormented spirit that glared out of bodily eyes, when *what seemed Ahab* rushed from his room, was for a time but a vacated thing, a formless somnambulistic being, a ray of living light, to be sure, but without an object to colour, and therefore a blankness in itself" (my italics).

ISHMAEL AND AHAB VIEW THE WHALE DIFFERENTLY

The meaning Ishmael finds in the white whale is obviously very different from any of Ahab's—and the difference is perhaps most briefly suggested by saying that to Ahab the white whale was a personification, a "pasteboard mask," or perhaps an effigy, of something otherwise unknown and unassailable; whereas to Ishmael the whale is merely a symbol. If afflicted with a monomania such as Ahab's, one can feel like assaulting and destroying a personification or effigy; but the only thing to do with a symbol is to understand it. Ishmael, therefore, saw the white whale as a symbol of what might be called a metaphysical hypothesis, and throughout the rest of the book he shows himself endeavouring to study the evidence for and against that hypothesis. He seeks not to destroy the whale for vengeance, profit, or pleasure, but simply to understand it, to comprehend it, to reduce the unknown to intelligibility. And this, he insists, is not a project to be pursued in a quiet study, ruminating over the partial and unreliable reports of other men (as provided in fragmentary books or faulty paintings of whales). As he puts it: "Only in the heart of quickest perils; only when within the eddyings of his angry flukes; only on the profound unbounded sea, can the fully invested whale be truly and livingly found out."

ISHMAEL IS THE MOST MOTIVATED TO UNDERSTAND THE WHALE

The fact has been strangely overlooked that Ishmael, as well as Ahab, deliberately embarked in quest of the white whale. The others aboard the *Pequod* were pursuing other ends when they were irresistibly drawn into Ahab's wake. But Ishmael tells us in the first chapter that "chief among these motives" which induced him into going a-whaling "was the overwhelming idea of the great whale himself. Such a portentous and mysterious monster roused all my curiosity . . . the great floodgates of the wonder-world swung open, and in the wild conceits that swayed me to my purpose, two and two there floated into my inmost soul, endless processions of the whale, and, mid most of them all, one grand hooded phantom, like a snow hill in the air."

This curiosity, or passion to comprehend, explains why it is Ishmael (not Ahab, Starbuck, or anyone else) who is shown as being interested in every detail about whales, both species and individuals—the whales that appear in books, pictures, and doorknockers; that contribute food, oil, and corset stays; that are detected in mountain ridges and stars; that have been fossilized, worshipped, hunted, and scientifically studied; that have been dissected, analysed, and described to exhibit every possible characteristic. Understandably enough, he often feels that complete comprehension is impossible—"there is no earthly way of finding out precisely what the whale really looks like"; "the mystic-marked whale remains undecipherable" and "dissect him how I may . . . I know him not, and never will." Nevertheless, he must continue to make the attempt "to approve myself omnisciently exhaustive in the enterprise," to pursue his "thoughts of this Leviathan" wherever they lead, through "the whole circle of the sciences, and all the generations of whales, and men, and mastodons, past, present, and to come, with all the revolving panoramas of empire on earth, and throughout the whole universe."

This necessity to learn and include everything in order to

comprehend the essential principle is the true artistic justification of Ishmael's compiling the mass of whaling details given in *Moby Dick*. He is attempting to see the whale not partially, as a personified malignancy, a natural peril, a challenge, or a monetary value, but omnisciently, as a possibly intelligible microcosm in a possibly intelligible cosmos. The meaning of the white whale, for Ishmael, seems to be either the totality or essential of all meanings—in a word, attainable only by omniscience.

The Meanings of the Sea

William Hamilton

In the following excerpt, William Hamilton explains the variety of meanings of the sea in *Moby-Dick*. In Hamilton's view, the land represents a sort of imprisonment, where people are trapped and share the same unchallenged beliefs. But at sea, individuals are offered a variety of viewpoints about the world and their place in it. However, to take advantage of that, Ishmael must first lose his romantic notion of the sea and accept it for what it truly is, both cruel and nurturing. Hamilton is a theologian and the author of *Reading* Moby-Dick *and Other Essays* and *New Essence of Christianity.* He hosted a nationally broadcast CBS television series devoted to explaining religion and theology.

[Literary critic] Henry A. Murray, our wisest Melvillean, has suggested that at the time of the writing of *Moby-Dick* Melville had begun to allow the forces of passion and the unconscious to dominate him, setting up an inner dualism that was to shape all the rest of his life and work. On one side, generally symbolized by "sea," lay the world of spirit: open space, freedom, danger, the heart, dedication, benevolence, God, and madness. On the other side (land or the city) was closed space, family, slavishness, safety, the head, rationality, self-interest, the world. Yes, but in *Moby-Dick* the sea is more than a single thing. It is home of both the nursing whale mothers and the sharks devouring each other's entrails. It is so eloquently serene that it can nearly heal Ahab's madness; and it is darkness and death. If the sea covers two-thirds of the earth, it also covers two-thirds of *Moby-Dick*—both redemption and damnation. . . .

William Hamilton, *Melville and the Gods.* Chico, CA: Scholars Press, 1985. Copyright © 1985 by Scholars Press. Reproduced by permission.

ISHMAEL'S ROMANTIC INTERPRETATION OF THE SEA

The full sea in *Moby-Dick* is the sea of Ishmael plus the sea of Ahab. Neither is simple. Ishmael begins in flight from oppressive land, fascinated by Bulkington's courageous landlessness. But he has new experiences. He stands masthead watches and has a look, from a distance, at Ahab and his sea. He becomes discontented with Bulkington's restlessness, for the world that is ever at sea has more evil and death in it than Ishmael wants.

Ahab's sea has no narrative development. It is unchanging and complex. He understands the humanizing sea, and once is even touchingly tempted by it. But character and vocation wed him to the inhuman sea, all madness and death.

Ishmael is elusive both as character and narrator. But we do know something about his sea, from the very beginning of the novel. Ishmael's land—in this case New York City—is boredom, depression, and even—half-seriously—suicidal. He goes to sea, he tells us, because he is in some kind of jeopardy and the sea can heal. Why otherwise do Manhattan dwellers wander down to river or sea on a Sunday afternoon? Meditation and water, everyone knows, are wedded forever, and *Moby-Dick* is partly a book about this wedding.

The closest Ishmael comes to explaining his feelings about the sea, and the closest Melville ever comes to the suggestion that there may be *a* clue to *Moby-Dick*, lies in the elusive remark about Narcissus [a myth about a Greek youth who fell in love with his reflection in the water], "who because he would not grasp the tormenting, mild image he saw in the fountain, plunged into it and was drowned." That image is the image we all see of ourselves in the water, and it is "the image of the ungraspable phantom of life; and this is the key to it all." Another modest divinization of the sea. The "true" Narcissus, of course, does not drown but pines away because he cannot possess the reflected beauty he sees in the water. Melville mythicizes the myth so that the meaning of "ungraspable" becomes drowning and death.

Ishmael went to sea to escape the threat of death in the life of the city. Yet the ocean itself is death-dealing—"there is death in this business of whaling." He abolishes his fear of the death of the sea by a conventionally pious (and unconvincing, perhaps even to him) affirmation of the soul's immortality. Upstate Presbyterianism, for a time, abolishes his fear of death on the water. Soon he will find that the water itself will abolish his fear of death on the land.

On the way to Nantucket, Ishmael continues his reflections on land and sea. Leaving the mainland, he reflects on "the intolerableness of all earthly effort"; he turns against what he calls the turnpike earth marked by slavish heels, and prepares "to admire the magnanimity of the sea which will permit no records." Land is death and despair; sea is also death, "monotonous and forbidding" and perhaps something more.

In chapter 16, a new note is added. Not only does sea heal the landsman's depression, not only is it the dangerous symbol of life ungraspable; now it is related to freedom, heroism, the idealized American character. Referring to the character of the Quaker, Ishmael remarks that sometimes a unique individual emerges

> who has also by the stillness and seclusion of many long nightwatches in the remote waters . . . been led to think untraditionally and independently; receiving all nature's sweet or savage impressions fresh from her own virgin, voluntary, and confiding breast, and thereby chiefly . . . to learn a bold and nervous lofty language—that man makes one in a whole nation's census—a mighty pageant creature, formed for noble tragedies.

Ishmael is thinking of Ahab, but Melville's voice may also be heard talking about the effect of the sea on his own struggle for a bold and nervous lofty language for the very book he is writing. Something in the sea brings out the human, tragic uniqueness in a man. This is one meaning of the wedding of meditation and water.

LAND REPRESENTS LACK OF FREEDOM

With this as background, Ishmael offers his tribute to his shipmate Bulkington who is at the helm as the *Pequod* leaves Nantucket. Ishmael will not finally be able to live wholly in the heroic air of Bulkington's radical landlessness (though Melville may have been so able), but here at the start of the voyage he longs to, as he struggles toward his maturity. Bulkington, just back from a long voyage, returns immediately to sea. "The land seemed scorching to his feet." Port he rejected—port as standing for help, friends, comfort, for "all that's kind to our mortalities." And Ishmael reflects on Bulkington's view of land and sea.

> But in that gale, the port, the land, is that ship's direst jeopardy; she must fly all hospitality; one touch of land though it

but graze the keel, would make her shudder through and through. With all her might she crowds all sail off shore; in so doing, fights 'gainst the very winds that fain would blow her homeward; seeks all the lashed sea's landlessness again; for refuge's sake forlornly rushing into peril; her only friend her bitterest foe!

This is a simple but astonishing allegory: ship is the soul, the wind is the world, land and home are peril, the sea's landlessness is freedom. And, Ishmael continues, "all deep earnest thinking is but the intrepid effort of the soul to keep the open independence of her sea; while the wildest winds of heaven and earth conspire to cast her on the treacherous, slavish shore." For in

landlessness alone resides the highest truth, shoreless, indefinite as God—so, better is it to perish in that howling infinite, than being gloriously dashed upon the lee, even if that were safety! For worm-like, then, oh! who would craven crawl to land!

This is the most deeply felt expression of Ishmael's naive idealization of the sea. Sea stands for all the heroic graces of humanity, while land, city, American history itself—all are rejected. Ishmael will always hold to this, but he will add to it. He has yet to encounter another's sea—that of his captain— and deeper waters await him. The intensity of these lines makes it hard to avoid the feeling that Melville put a very central part of his own imagination into this tribute to Bulkington and to landlessness as perhaps the only true divinity.

ISHMAEL LOSES HIS ROMANTIC VIEW OF THE SEA

Ishmael never loses his confidence in the healing sea, and he never rejects Bulkington. But in recounting his experience of standing masthead watch, he comes to see that the beautiful sea can be deadlier than the wild one. Up there, a hundred feet above the deck, you are "lost in the infinite series of the sea," the seductive sea, he calls it, where "everything resolves into languor." He recounts something like a classical mystical experience, as one is "lulled into such an opium-like listlessness of vacant, unconscious reverie" that he "loses his identity, takes the mystic ocean at his feet for the visible image of that deep, blue, bottomless soul, pervading mankind and nature"; lulled by the "inscrutable tides of God," one is likely to "drop through that transparent air into the summer sea, no more to rise for ever." This new dimension of Ishmael's sea, this curious affinity between water, beauty, death and mystic selflessness, is summarized in a striking passage.

> Death is only a launching into the region of the strange Untried; it is but the first salutation to the possibilities of the immense Remote, the Wild, the Watery, the Unshored; therefore, to be death-longing eyes of such men, who still have left in them some interior compunctions against suicide, does the all-contributed and all-receptive ocean alluringly spread forth his whole plain of unimaginable, taking terrors, and wonderful, new-life adventures; and from the hearts of infinite Pacifics, the thousand mermaids sing to them—"Come hither, broken-hearted; here is another life without the guilt of intermediate death; here are wonders supernatural, without dying for them. Come hither! bury thyself in a life which, to your now equally abhorred and abhorring, landed world, is more oblivious than death. Come hither! put up *thy* gravestone, too, within the churchyard, and come hither, till we marry thee!"

Ishmael has discovered not only the literal death that lurks in the craft of whaling, but the deeper mystical death that lurks beneath the whole romantic attitude to nature. Melville's Narcissus dies in the water because, in his egotism, he wishes to merge with the image of himself in the water. Ahab dies, and brings others to their deaths, for the same mad reason. Ishmael begins to see this madness of mysticism, and this discernment will give him his freedom from both madness and death in Ahab's sea.

Sea-mysticism taught Ishmael something, but it didn't convert him. He had gone to sea because of death on the land, and he knew that he would be exploring death at sea. He may still be drawn to Bulkington's landlessness, but he is becoming as grimly realistic about sea as he had been about land. He is presumably prepared to confront the spiritual temptation offered by his captain, and in response to that, a new factor emerges in his reflection on land and sea. He comes to long for the land at sea, much as he had longed for the sea from the land.

ISHMAEL ACKNOWLEDGES THE SEA'S DESTRUCTIVE POWERS

Let us look at this emerging realism. The best example can be found in chapter 58, "Brit." The chapter begins with a comparison of the brit-strewn ocean to an American wheat field, reminding us of the connection Melville liked to draw between ocean and prairie. But this comparison leads not to the healing sea with which he began, and not to any praise of heroic landlessness. It leads to an expansion of his mast-head pessimism, as Ishmael remarks that

> the most terrific of all mortal disasters have immemorially and indiscriminately befallen tens and hundreds of thousands of those who have gone upon the waters . . .

He had spoken before of the sea's "unshored, harborless immensities" and he had noted, in the chapter on whiteness, the special terror of white water. But these earlier explorations are made more precise. The destructiveness of the sea is used to attack American pride. However much, Ishmael says, baby man may congratulate himself on his technological prowess, "the sea will insult and murder him," for American self-righteousness ignores "the full awfulness of the sea."

Chapter 58 is the decisive summary of Ishmael's engagement with the inhuman sea as an experienced sailor. "The live sea swallows up ships and crews," it is like "a savage tigress" or "mad battle steed"; the "masterless ocean" (masterless, in that no guiding providence constrains it) in its "devilish brilliance and beauty" destroys all. And finally: "Consider, once more, the universal cannibalism of the sea." This cannibalism is shortly explored visually in the scene of the sharks devouring their own entrails and in Queequeg's comment on that scene: "de god wat made shark must be one dam Ingin." The presence of death, even in the mildest of seas, is beautifully portrayed in the picture of the beheaded carcass of the whale, released from the ship's side.

> Beneath the unclouded and mild azure sky, upon the fair face of the pleasant sea, wafted by the joyous breezes, that great mass of death floats on and on, till lost in infinite perspectives.

And in "The Try-Works" chapter, the *Pequod* becomes a flaming hell, sailing into "the blackness of the sea," that sea thus transformed into "the dark side of this earth."

ISHMAEL CHANGES HIS OPINION OF LAND

The mature Ishmael's perception of the sea's evil leads him to modify the passionate landlessness he had earlier admired in Bulkington. Since the sea is a cannibal, perhaps the contrasting land is not quite so "turnpike," so contemptible. In a statement more like Tommo, at the beginning of *Typee*, than his own early romantic optimism, he can say:

> For as this appalling ocean surrounds the verdant land, so in the soul of man there lies one insular Tahiti full of peace and joy, but encompassed by all the horrors of the half known life.

> God keep thee! Push not off from that isle [the inner isle, of
> course, but also those other isles Ishmael has pushed off
> from: Manhattan, Nantucket], thou canst never return!

This identification of the soul's inner security with land is
something new for Ishmael. It is not that he has become a
landsman, and he is not utterly rejecting romantic landlessness, but the simple distinction between the evil land and
the healing sea is certainly blurred.

THE PACIFIC OCEAN AS A SYMBOL OF THE UNIVERSE

Ishmael has one more dimension of the sea to discover. He
has yet to encounter the Pacific. Earlier he had told us that
the Atlantic is settled and civilized, while the Pacific is "solitary and savage." At the close of the novel, as the *Pequod* finally enters the Pacific waters, Ishmael utters a final credo
(in chapter 111, which [literary critic] F. O. Matthiessen has
called Melville's greatest):

> There is, one knows not what sweet mystery about this sea,
> whose gently awful stirrings seem to speak of some hidden
> soul beneath . . . And meet it is, that over these sea-pastures,
> wide-rolling watery prairies and Potters' fields of all four
> continents, the waves should rise and fall, and ebb and flow
> unceasingly; for here, millions of mixed shapes and shadows,
> drowned dreams, somnambulisms, reveries; all that we call
> lives and souls, lie dreaming, dreaming, still; tossing like
> slumberers in their beds; the ever rolling waves but made so
> by their restlessness.

Here the sea is the *anima mundi* [a vital force permeating
the world], the very principle of life itself, restless as life is,
gentle and deadly. And again, in yet another sense, the Pacific has become a god.

> To any meditative Magian rover, this serene Pacific, once be-
> held, must ever after be the sea of his adoption. It rolls the
> mid-most waters of the world, the Indian ocean and Atlantic
> being but its arms. The same waves wash the moles of the
> new-built California towns, but yesterday planted by the re-
> centest race of men, and lave the faded but still gorgeous
> skirts of Asiatic lands older than Abraham; while all between
> float milky-ways of coral isles, and low-lying, endless, un-
> known Archipelagoes, and impenetrable Japans. Thus this
> mysterious, divine Pacific zones the world's whole bulk
> about; makes all coasts one bay to it; seems the tide-beating
> heart of earth. Lifted by those eternal swells, you needs must
> own the seductive god, bowing your head to Pan.

Ishmael's sea ends as it begins, with divinity. At the beginning of *Moby-Dick* the sea is a minor god, Narcissus. Here,

at the close, the mighty Pacific has become a symbol of the entire universe, heaven and earth together. Pan [Greek deity noted for lustful behavior] instead of Narcissus, before whom all must bow. Melville finally could not laud the Christian God because he came to believe him to be evil. The sea is his new god who does not lose his divinity because of his evil. Ahab's sea will prove to be a confirmation of that Pacific Ocean that Ishmael was tempted to worship.

In chapter 114, "The Glider," the *Pequod* is at the Japanese fishing grounds, in the Pacific, and the weather is mild. Ishmael reverts briefly to his masthead romanticism, and speaks of the stillness created by "the tranquil beauty and brilliance of the ocean's skin" that almost tempts him to forget the tiger heart, the velvet paw concealing the deadly fang. It is interesting to note that he describes his experience of the ocean's beauty as a "land-like feeling," reflecting his recent rediscovery of the land.

This serene Pacific even affects Ahab, as he draws closer to his engagement with the white whale. Earlier, in a meditation, he had felt the healing of the sea: "the warm waves blush like wine," he had admitted, but they could not heal him then. He is too demoniac, madness maddened. Here, at the journey's end, Ahab expresses the same longing. "Would to God these blessed calms would last," he says to himself. But they cannot; storms follow calms, death is life's only secret.

AHAB VIEWS THE SEA AS BEING EVIL

In chapter 70, Ahab speaks to the decapitated head of a whale, lying against the ship's side. He asks the whale for its secret, identifying with him in his deep diving and familiarity with the "bones of millions of the drowned."

> Thou hast been where bell or diver never went; hast slept by many a sailor's side, where sleepless mothers would give their lives to lay them down. Thou saw'st the locked lovers when leaping from their flaming ship; heart to heart they sank beneath the exulting wave; true to each other, when heaven seemed false to them. Thou saw'st the murdered mate when tossed by pirates from the midnight deck; for hours he fell into the deeper midnight of the insatiate maw; and his murderers still sailed on unharmed—while swift lightnings shivered the neighboring ship that would have borne a righteous husband to outstretched, longing arms.

And then, Ahab concludes—unable, like Melville, to think of evil without also thinking of faith.

> O head! thou hast seen enough to split the planets and make
> an infidel of Abraham. . .

Ahab knows what the whale knows, and the whale knows
that the sea is inexplicably evil, like the world itself. Ahab,
the perfect Transcendentalist [a philosophy in which it is believed that the divine is the guiding principle in human be-
havior], knows that nature is not itself, but only a mask cov-
ering what lies in the human soul. Nature and soul are one;
whale-head and Ahab are one. So in addressing the head, he
is really addressing himself, and it is fitting that the address
to the head should conclude with his most heartfelt tribute
to the symbolic nature of language.

> O Nature, and O soul of man! how far beyond all utterance
> are your linked analogies! not the smallest atom stirs or lives
> in matter, but has its cunning duplicate in mind.

Later, in a similar meditative scene, Ahab watches a dying whale turn toward the sun, and his language to the
whale and to the sea becomes virtually a prayer. (It is interesting that both Ishmael and Ahab have a divine sea at the
heart of their stories.)

> Oh, thou dark Hindoo half of nature, who of drowned bones
> hast builded thy separate throne somewhere in the heart of
> these unverdured seas; thou art an infidel, thou queen, and
> too truly speakest to me in the wide-slaughtering typhoon,
> and the hushed burial of its after calm. . . . In vain, oh whale,
> dost thou seek intercedings with yon all quickening sun, that
> only calls forth life, but gives it not again. Yet dost thou, darker
> half, rock me with a prouder, if a darker faith. All thy unnam-
> able imminglings float beneath me here; I am buoyed by
> breaths of once living things, exhaled as air, but water now.
>
> Then hail, for ever hail, O sea, in whose eternal tossings the
> wild fowl finds his only rest. Born of earth, yet suckled by the
> sea; though hill and valley mothered me, ye billows are my
> foster-brothers!

Ahab, like Ishmael, turns to paganism to find the right words
of praise; not to Pan, but to the even older chthonic goddess
of the waters. Ahab has become one with that divinity, far
more radically than ever Ishmael had done with his divini-
ties on the masthead.

Once more, before the chase, Ahab confronts his goddess
in the forms of the gentle Pacific. Chapter 132, "The Symphony," begins with a striking comparison of the sea and
sky. Both are blue, yet

> the pensive air was transparently pure and soft, with a woman's

look, and the robust and man-like sea heaved with long, strong, lingering swells . . .

Birds become the thoughts of the feminine air, while whales, sword-fish and sharks are the thoughts—the realities—of the masculine sea. The sexual imagery in this union of sea and sky becomes even more explicit.

> Aloft, like a royal czar and king, the sun seemed giving this gentle air to this bold and rolling sea; even as a bride to groom. And at the girdling line of the horizon, a soft and tremulous motion—most seen here at the equator—denoted the fond, throbbing trust, the loving alarms, with which the poor bride gave her bosom away.

Ahab is affected by this brilliant blue morning, with its union of sea and sky. He thinks of his children, and the enchanted, feminine air "did at last seem to dispel, for a moment, the cankerous things in his soul." He looks into the water and sees his own reflection, but not his madness and anger. He weeps and seems, for a moment, wholly sane. He admits to Starbuck that he has forsaken the peaceful land "to make war on the horrors of the deep." But the feminine air loses her struggle with the man who once declared that he knew not a mother, and the murdering masculine sea wins this decisive last battle. Ahab admits to Starbuck that he cannot relinquish the search, for he does not think his own thoughts, but God's. As Ishmael once and briefly lost his soul to the water, here is Ahab losing his utterly, becoming one with the water he sails upon. He has taken upon himself its murderous humanity, rejecting the softening claims of sky and land. In this single act he has become suicide, murderer, madman, god. Romantic transcendentalism received no more decisive rejection in the nineteenth century than in this story of Ahab and his sea. By the same token, the account of Pip's madness is just as decisive a rejection of Protestant orthodoxy. In the water for hours, Pip discovered that God was in control, that He was evil, and that the invisible spheres were truly formed in fright.

Moby-Dick is found, all hands save Ishmael are lost, and the *Pequod*, rammed by the whale, sinks into the vortex. At the end, "the great shroud of the sea rolled on as it rolled five thousand years ago" when God, in his anger, set out to destroy the world by flood. At the end, there is only Ishmael and the sea.

CHAPTER 3

The Use of
Religion in
Moby-Dick

Viewing *Moby-Dick* as a Sacred Text

Lawrence Buell

Lawrence Buell contends that Melville uses specific narrative techniques to establish *Moby-Dick* as a surrogate sacred text in response to a nineteenth-century American call for secular priests. Buell argues that many artists and intellectuals of the time, including Melville, were reacting against what they considered to be the confining moral teachings of Christianity. By exploring the same moral themes as the Bible, these artists sought to offer an alternative moral view of the world. Professor Buell teaches literature at Harvard University and is the author of many books and articles on nineteenth-century American literature, including *New England Literary Culture: From Revolution Through Renaissance.*

In certain ways *Moby-Dick is* a sort of scripture. It is, to begin with, indisputably one of the works of the American literary "canon," as scholars like to call it, read and taught by the professorial priesthood [meaning literary scholars] with a more genuinely religious zeal than most of that priesthood probably feel toward the literal sacred texts of their own ethnic traditions—the Torah, the New Testament, or whatever. In my field, to write a commentary on *Moby-Dick* is more respectable than to write a commentary on the book of Job or Jonah. One reason for this is the depth of the waters in which Melville fished, the fact that this particular fish story becomes ultimately in some sense a record of an encounter with the divine. The book's language is drenched in sacramentalism, "brimming over with signals of the transcendent." When the white whale rises out of the water on the first day of the chase, it does not merely breach: "the grand god revealed himself" (Chap. 133). Here and at innumerable

Lawrence Buell, "*Moby-Dick* as Sacred Text," *New Essays on* Moby-Dick, edited by Richard H. Brodhead. New York: Cambridge University Press, 1986. Copyright © 1986 by Cambridge University Press. Reproduced by permission of the publisher and the author.

other points metaphor seems to convert story into myth.

[According to Melville scholar H. Bruce Franklin,] "Despite all the heterodoxy [not orthodox] of opinion on *Moby-Dick*, few critics doubt that Moby Dick is a god." Taken literally, that critical statement seems bizarre, especially in light of studies, during the two decades since it was made, that have placed much emphasis on how the world of *Moby-Dick* communicates to the reader through the filter of "Ishmael's quandaries as both neophyte whaleman and retrospective narrator" as to "whether the White Whale is simply a naturalistic whale or whether he is a creature of supernatural properties." The book can even be read as a gigantic spoof of the sacred imagination from animism [the attribution of a living soul to inanimate objects, plants, etc.] (Ishmael measuring the whale's skeleton in the Arsacides in the face of horrified priestly opposition) to the Bible itself (the credibility of the Book of Jonah uproariously sabotaged in Chapter 83 under the guise of defense). . . . So suffused with indeterminacy and satire is the book that to read it simply as a work of prophetic witness would be to commit an oversimplification parallel to Ahab's oversimplification of the meaning of the voyage. Yet . . . the sense of the sacred with which the world of the book and particularly the figure of the white whale are infused never evaporates, but on the contrary continues to be resuggested even as it is questioned. . . .

A NEW IDEA OF WRITER AS SECULAR PRIEST

One of the major intellectual forces behind the whole so-called American literary renaissance to which Melville's work contributed was . . . the breakdown of biblical authority in Protestant America. This had both "negative" and "positive" aspects. Negatively, the rise of the "higher criticism" in biblical studies, which began to make significant inroads in America during the decade of Melville's birth, seemed threatening and destructive in its approach to the Bible (and, by extension, to institutionalized Christianity as a whole) as a culture-bound, historical artifact subject to the same methods of interpretation and susceptible to the same errors and obsolescence as any other ancient artifact. This threatened to reduce holy scripture to myth in the bad sense—to quaint superstitious fabrication. Concomitantly, however, a less parochial and more creative understanding of the religious imagination now became possible, an affirmative reading of myth as the expression of spiritual archetypes informing not only the Bible but the scriptures of all cultures, and not only ancient texts but—at least potentially—the literature of one's own day as well. At least partially offsetting the disillusioning sense that prophets were no more than poets was the exciting dream that poets might be prophets. This indeed was one of the great themes of the romantic movement in both England and America. It was wholly in keeping with this thrust of romanticism that its first major American exemplar, [nineteenth-century American poet and philosopher] Ralph Waldo Emerson, was an ex-minister who, in reaction against contemporary theology and denominationalism, turned to the vocation of freelance lecturer-writer, defining it as a secular priesthood. Emerson's scattered comments bearing on the relation between poetry and prophecy provide the best American statement of how the demythologizing of Judeo-Christianity could give rise to creative remythologizing as well as to simple negation. . . .

Emerson's fundamental argument is simple: The acceptance of Jesus's authority over us, on which institutionalized Christianity is based, represents a false crystallization of Jesus's figurative speech ("this high chant from the poet's lips"), the true intent of which was not merely to say "I am divine" but that "God incarnates himself in man, and evermore goes forth anew to take possession of his world." Hence "Christianity became a Mythus, as the poetic teaching of Greece and of Egypt, before." To be true to the prophetic message that institutionalization has occluded, the preacher of today must therefore not be a custodian but a "bard of the Holy Ghost" who, through his own prophetic utterance, will "acquaint men at first hand with Deity.". . .

Emerson's dream that today's verbal artists, be they preachers or poets, might speak with prophetic authority was powerfully appealing to his age as a whole, which saw the production of at least one new Bible (*The Book of Mormon*) and two epoch-making literary works that laid direct claim to divine inspiration: [nineteenth-century American novelist] Harriet Beecher Stowe's *Uncle Tom's Cabin* and [nineteenth-century American poet] Walt Whitman's *Leaves of Grass*. Melville's writing clearly also reflects this dream both in taking aim at the theological status quo and in using fiction (and later poetry) as vehicles for reflecting on the range of ultimate questions with which the Bible itself is preoccupied. . . .

Techniques Used to Make the Whale a Religious Symbol

[Melville's] general orientation is aptly characterized by [literary critic] Robert Richardson as "mythic investiture": the infusion of what we know to be natural phenomena with a sense of mystic otherness. "Although we never lose sight of the fact that Moby Dick is simply a large albino sperm whale, it is, from the start, the *idea* of the great whale that compels us as it compels Ishmael. . . . We see the whale through a veil of rumor, scholarship, legend, and myth; by imperceptible degrees we come to acquiesce in the appropriateness of such things, and we eventually find ourselves regarding the whale as something more than a whale." Richardson's "simply" strikes me as narrowing the range of options the text keeps open, but otherwise this is an admirable summation. What is especially interesting and distinctive about the investiture process is how the narrative builds this impression in the face of the narrator's disclaimers and even discreditation. A convenient example is Chapter 86, "The Tail," convenient for being an almost paradigmatic [an example or pattern] illustration of how the cetology chapters in general work. All interweave most of the following elements:

1. A substratum of cetological data, testifying to the American—and Melvillean—passion for "informative" unfamiliar lore ("the compact round body of its root expands into two broad, firm, flat palms or flukes").

2. Rhetorical intensification of the data ("Could annihilation occur to matter, this were the thing to do it").

3. Metaphorization of the data, so as to begin to dissolve the shipboard context (a series of comparisons between the whale's tail and the elephant's trunk).

4. Mythification of the data ("Out of the bottomless profundities the gigantic tail seems spasmodically snatching at the highest heaven. So in dreams, have I seen majestic Satan thrusting forth his tormented colossal claw from the flame Baltic of Hell").

5. Complication of the mythic framework so as to introduce the possibility of solipsism [the view that the self is all that exists or can be known] ("But in gazing at such scenes, it is all in all what mood you are in; if in the Dantean [referring to fourteenth-century Italian poet Dante Alighieri, author of *The Divine Comedy*], the devils will occur to you; if in that of Isaiah, the archangels").

6. Comic disruption of the mythic framework (the tongue-in-cheek image of whales "praying" with peaked flukes like "the military elephants of antiquity" that, according to Ishmael's source, "often hailed the morning with their trunks uplifted in the profoundest silence").

7. Self-conscious proclamation of scribal inadequacy ("The more I consider this mighty tail, the more do I deplore my inability to express it").

8. Ambiguous reformulation of the whale as mystery ("Dissect him how I may, then, I but go skin deep; I know him not, and never will. But if I know not even the tail of this whale, how understand his head? much more, how comprehend his face, when he has none? Thou shalt see my back parts, my tail, he seems to say, but my face shall not be seen. But I cannot completely make out his back parts; and hint what he will about his face, I say again he has no face").

This last gesture, with which the chapter ends, is particularly suggestive. It teeters on the edge of comic absurdity, with the (deliberately?) lame puns "I go but skin deep" and "the tail of this whale," and with the (whimsically? mischievously?) hyperbolic appropriation of Yahweh's warning to Moses on Horeb (Exodus 34:23): "thou shalt see my back parts: but my face shall not be seen" (King James version). Yet coming on top of Satan, the archangels, and so forth, and in the context of practical documentation of the whale's power and inscrutability, the gesture of divination also makes dramatic sense. To the extent that we hear the former note, we shall read the passage and Ishmael's discourses generally as testifying to the quixoticism [exaggeratedly romantic] of the myth-making process; and we shall want to ascribe to Melville or at least to Ishmael the debunking conception of myth as fabrication. This leads, on the level of symbol interpretation, to a reading of *Moby-Dick* as an allegory of reading and particularly as an allegory of unreadability: the undecipherability of the whale as text. . . . This response leads ultimately to a reading of *Moby-Dick* as about an encounter with the realm of the transcendent that dramatizes parallel failures of human striving (Ahab) and knowing (Ishamel). In this reading, Ishmaelean mockery of the kind just noted starts to look like self-protective compensation for the frustration and anxiety of failing to grasp the elusive, mysterious, and therefore threatening Other. It is through the eyes of this second reading that *Moby-Dick* begins to look somewhat like a sacred text.

NARRATIVE STRUCTURE SUGGESTS SACRED TEXT

That this second reading is more persuasive as well as more powerful than the first is strongly suggested by the book's narrative structure. The narrative "proves" Ahab to have been a false prophet, but it does not disown the framework of supernaturalism established by his shadow Fedallah's three [William Shakespeare's tragedy] *Macbeth*-like prophecies, which uncannily come to pass. The narrative leaves open the question of whether the White Whale is a divine or demonic agent, and in leaving this question open leaves us in a state of wonder rather than with a confident reduction of the whale to the status of material object or (on the symbolic level) narcissistic projection. Particularly interesting in this regard is the first closeup of Moby Dick:

> Not the white bull Jupiter swimming away with ravished Europa clinging to his graceful horns; his lovely, leering eyes sideways intent upon the maid; with smooth bewitching fleetness, rippling straight for the nuptial bower in Crete; not Jove, not that great majesty Supreme! did surpass the glorified White Whale as he so divinely swam (Chap. 133)

Franklin rightly calls this "one of the great moments of revelation in literature." Not that we should yield to the temptation of concluding "Aha! this *proves* that Melville thinks Moby Dick is a god—be he agent or principal." The passage doesn't quite do that. As an epic simile, it advertises itself as possibly "only" a literary device, as a device that beautifies rhetoric by infusing a dose of classical decor, thereby betraying consciousness of artifice in the midst of worshipful enthusiasm. . . .

The reader of *Moby-Dick* is all the more eager to experience the White Whale's appearance as apocalyptic after such long foreshadowing—after hundreds of premonitory references to the "grand hooded phantom, like a snow hill in the air" (Chap. 1). Here the book plays an interesting double game. Because its central subject is an absent object of obsession for nearly the entire narrative, the text continually signals to the reader that "This is not yet quite reality; this is only preparatory information or interpretation." Not until a third of the book is over does an encounter with even an ordinary whale take place. During this long buildup, the repetitous quality of the cetology chapters and of Ishmael's meditations in general, combined with the fundamental fact of Moby Dick's absence, reinforce the plausibility of the frequent hints that the quest is empty of meaning except for what is read into it. On the basis of what we are allowed to see, nothing is easier than to subscribe to Ishmael's mock lament:

> How vain and foolish, then, thought I, for timid untravelled man to try to comprehend aright this wondrous whale, by merely poring over his dead attenuated skeleton. (Chap. 103)

—a complaint that applies both to the idolatrous devotion of the Arsacidean [Iranian dynasty that ruled from 247 B.C. to A.D. 224] priests and to Ishmael's whole project of trying to construct a symbolic edifice from the whale's various body parts. Nothing is easier at this point than to accept Ishmael's revision of Ahab's reading of "The Whiteness of the Whale," according to which Ishmael does not precisely reject Ahab's theory of Moby Dick as malignant so much as reconceive his balefulness in terms of cosmic blankness or meaningless-ness ("a colorless, all-color of atheism from which we shrink" [Chap. 42]), as opposed to purposive ill, thus depriv-ing the sense of evil of any coherence or plan. At the same time, the plethora of foreshadowings and the repeated ad-missions of intellectual defeat and skepticism create intense frustration for the reader as well as the narrator (as every teacher of undergraduates knows) and with this a great longing for closure, which the text in the long run pretty much provides. Near the end, the narrative becomes much more linear; the whale's eruption into the text and disposal of the *Pequod* dissipates the haze of speculation in the sense of providing a resolution, at least on the plot level, to the prior state of indefiniteness. In this sense, [literary critic] Bainard Cowan is precisely right in claiming that "the final events of the book do away with ambiguity and determine all meaning toward one end." The narrative structure is remi-niscent of the tale of Job without the frame. In each work, re-dundant expostulation and soul searching build up to an in-tolerable pitch of uncertainty until abruptly resolved by authoritative, repressive intervention—except that in Mel-ville the whale speaks only on the level of action. . . .

The status of what I have called the apocalypse of the White Whale can be clarified further with the aid of [literary critic] Paul Ricoeur's . . . [belief that] as a textual phenome-non, revelation . . . [is a] compound of overlapping forms of discourse . . . prophetic, narrative, prescriptive, wisdom, and hymnic. All five, I think, can be detected in *Moby-Dick*, but only the first two need concern us here. The mark of the first is "the idea of a double author of speech and writing. Revelation is the speech of another," that is, God, "behind the speech of the prophet." In *Moby-Dick* Ahab's discourse claims the equivalent of this, but not Ishmael's. Ahab claims to speak as "the Fates' lieutenant" (Chap. 134). To be sure, his notion of "right worship" is "defiance" (Chap. 119), and in this he extends an occasional biblical trait of prophetic behavior (compare the will to deviance in Jeremiah and Jonah) and makes it his norm, arrogating prophetic power entirely to himself. What allows him to see his speech as having prophetic authority, however, is that his perceptions have a more than personal validity. On the Quarter-deck, for instance, he justifies pursuit of Moby Dick not merely for the sake of vengeance but because "Truth hath no confines" (Chap. 36). Vengeance must be justified in terms of some cosmic scheme. Ahab's "discourse of revelation," however, is of course made in the long run to seem a perversion of the real thing by being enclosed within Ishmael's, which makes no such pretense, even if at times it gestures faintly in that direction, as when Ishmael seriocomically announces his voyage as part of "the grand programme of Providence" (Chap. 1). Viewed as prophetic utterance, then, *Moby-Dick* presents a kind of antiscripture (Ahab's discourses) within a secularized and on the whole debunking commentary.

NARRATIVE AS SACRED REVELATION

Conceived as revelation *narrative*, however, the scriptural status of *Moby-Dick* looks rather different. "What is essential in the case of narrative discourse," observes Ricoeur, "is the emphasis on the founding event or events as the imprint, mark, or trace of God's act. Confession takes place through narration, and the problematic of inspiration is in no way the primary consideration. God's mark is in history before being in speech. It is only secondarily in speech inasmuch as this history itself is brought to language in the speech-act of narration." Insofar as the *Pequod*'s encounter with the monster of the deep is a mysterious, deeply inexplicable, and magic-suggesting event that gives rise to the telling of the story in the first place and also, at the end of the tale, supersedes the telling in the sense that reflective commentary becomes largely displaced by the force of the narrative relation—insofar as all this is true, *Moby-Dick* begins to reemerge on the narrative level as sacred text even as it might have seemed that any pretenses to revelation had been contained by wily Ishmael. I take it that one of the reasons, maybe the main reason, for the inconsistency of Ishmael's disappearance from the later stages of the narrative may be to dramatize this very effect: the effect of what seems *comparatively* like a pure, unmediated vision of successive mysterious events bursting through the power of both commentary (Ishmael) and false prophecy (Ahab) to contain them. It is interesting in this regard that when Ishmael does reappear in the Epilogue, he seems to have been coopted by the discourse of revelation. He now speaks in the role of Job's messenger-servant, whose function is simply to serve as the reporter of the demonically arranged and divinely permitted catastrophe: "I only am escaped alone to tell thee" (Epilogue). . . .

Numerous critics have noted that the use of dual foci in the novel—Ishmael the speculator and Ahab the actor—sets up a tension and a symbiosis between circular and linear thinking. [Literary critic] Robert Caserio has extended this insight in a discerning analysis of Melvillean plotting that will be helpful here. "Melville dramatizes himself through Ishmael," notes Caserio, "as not actively telling or willfully writing his story and its ending. As an author and agent he, like his hero, wants to be seen as thrown clear of his work, as passive, himself at the mercy of the instability that 'features' event. This is his way of proving he is not the story's dictator, an Ahab-like sultanist of the brain." The context of this observation is an extended analogy between Ahab as a representative of old-fashioned nineteenth-century realistic conceptions of linear plotting, and Melville through Ishmael as moving toward a modern form of open, circuitous, experimental, inconclusive plotting, which for Caserio correlates with a shift from activism to quietism in political ideology. I agree with most of this shrewd diagnosis but would qualify it by adding that Ishmael's abdication of authority and the text's ultimate suspension or at least minimization of Ishmael as a narrative presence may be seen as done not just in the interest of countering the Ahabian single vision but, beyond that, as a means of recovering at least the possibility of a providential event structure, which the text introduces when the White Whale swims apocalyptically into the book and brings it to an abrupt but tidy close at the narrative level. Just as Ahab's liberties with political authority must not go unchastised, so Ishmael's liberties as discursive narrator must be rectified by resort to a linear revelation narrative—a linear narrative, at any rate, that continues to hold forth the possibility that a more than merely literary revelation has taken place.

The prospect of the authority of revelation at the prophetic level, eroded by Ishmael's critique of Ahab, is thus partially recovered at the level of plot through the agency of the whale and through the move toward greater objectification of the narrative voice. The narrative method of having the tale eventually seem to reabsorb and outstrip its teller reflects and repeats the romantic impulse both to demythologize and remythologize. In this it reflects, but with a difference, Emerson's dictum to the newborn bards of the Holy Ghost to "cast behind you all conformity, and acquaint men at first hand with Deity." The *form* of this prescription is enacted faithfully in *Moby-Dick* by Ishmael's exposure of the arbitrariness of all particular readings of the divine (starting with the juxtaposition of Father Mapple-ism and Yojo worship as equivalent rituals) in a narrative pattern in which all speculation about the divine is abruptly displaced by the revelation of that which might actually be a mark of the divine. Yet then again, it might not. This is Melville's aesthetics of doubt; and as every Melvillean knows, the issue becomes progressively more clouded and doubtful in Melville's later novels, *Pierre* and *The Confidence-Man.* . . .

MOBY-DICK REFLECTS NEW DEMOCRATIC VIEW OF RELIGIONS

To the extent that *Moby-Dick* verges on revelation, what brand of revelation does it provide? [Literary critic] T. Walter Herbert makes a strong case for the dominance of a particular ethnic strand in Melvillean thinking. "Melville," writes Herbert, "sets forth a Calvinistic analysis of Ahab's moral strife in order to form a drama in which Calvin's God appears morally odious on liberal principles, yet in which liberal principles lose their validity as a description of religious truth," inasmuch as the wonder world through which the *Pequod* sails seems to operate more according to the orthodox vision of terror ("the invisible spheres were formed in fright" [Chap. 42]) than in terms of the liberal vision of meliorism [a doctrine that the world may be improved through human effort] and hope. . . . Melville looks like a conservative counterpart of Walt Whitman, both being concerned to make their images of deity as comprehensively syncretistic [unifying different schools of thought] as they can. Whitman is generally disposed to read those disparate traditions more affirmatively, as foreshadowing the new dispensation that he now proclaims, whereas Melville is more apt to play the graven images off against each other in mockery. Both, however, strive to use their ethnicity in "democratic" fashion, by converting an awareness of the ethnocentrism [evaluating other races and cultures by criteria specific to one's own] of particular scenarios and imagings of revelation into scenarios and imagings that might serve as models, positive or negative, for all the religions of the world. In this sense, *Moby-Dick*, along with [Whitman's collection of poetry] *Leaves of Grass*, stands as a great pioneering work of comparative religion and as one of the most ambitious products of the religious imagination that American literature is likely to produce.

The Epilogue Presents a Hindu View of Life

H.B. Kulkarni

H.B. Kulkarni traces how the structure of *Moby-Dick*'s epilogue coincides with the Hindu view of the life cycle of rebirth. Kulkarni retells Hindu mythology and parallels the plot with Melville's novel. He then shows how this plot also parallels the deeper theme of rebirth following destruction, in this case the rebirth of Ishmael following the destruction of the *Pequod.* Kulkarni is also the author of *Stephen Spender: An Annotated Bibliography.*

The dominant idea of the "Epilogue" is expressed in the image of the wheel and the vortex, connecting the story of Ixion and Job with the fate of Ishmael and indirectly of Ahab and his crew. Ishmael and the coffin which has been turned into a life-buoy are thrust upward from the "vital center" of the sea, and Ishmael is saved from drowning. If the wheel to which Ixion is tied is a wheel of fortune, Melville unites the two wheels, as it were, into one image of the vortex from the destructive rotation of which Ishmael is brought to life and begins to float upon what was once a coffin but has now been transformed into a life-saver. Like the coffin-life-buoy, the vortex too carries the double connotation of destruction and creation. The Hindu concept of the wheel contains both these connotations. It is the wheel of birth, death, and rebirth to which man is tied. It is in a sense a misfortune that man should be bound to this eternal process of life, an escape from which is regarded as the highest end of human existence. But it is also a matter of good fortune that the cyclical nature of existence makes death not the end but the beginning of a new life. Therefore it is possible to say that the Hebrew and Greek myths are united in the Hindu concept of the wheel of life which is based on the resolution of

H.B. Kulkarni, Moby-Dick: *A Hindu Avatar, a Study of Hindu Myth and Thought in* Moby-Dick. Logan: Utah State University Press, 1970. Copyright © 1970 by Utah State University. Reproduced by permission.

the paradox of reward and punishment, fortune and misfortune, and finally, of the paradox of life and death.

The images of the vortex and the wheel are made to suggest life emerging out of death and connect the survival of Ishmael with the death of Ahab and his crew by what is described as the Deluge itself. It has been pointed out how Ahab has been identified with the crew, the ship, and sometimes the whole of humanity. Equally extensive is the representative character of Ishmael. Some critics have called him "Everyman." Indeed he does project himself into the characters and situations of the novel and becomes their philosophic spokesman. If in Ahab, humanity seems to meet its end as in the mythical Flood, the cycle of life makes its new beginning in Ishmael. The end of one cycle and the beginning of another is symbolically connected with the myth of [a Hindu god] Vishnu which is the center of the Hindu view of life as an eternal cyclical process.

THE SINKING OF THE SHIP REPRESENTS REBIRTH

Vishnu dissolves the universe by submerging it in water on the surface of which he then reclines in a death-like state of trance. Later, he produces Brahma out of the lotus of his navel and commands him to create life again. This recreation of life out of Vishnu's navel is suggested in the image of the "button-like bubble." It represents the "vital center" of the sea and the hub of the rotating wheel of life, which bursts upward and brings forth a life-buoy to save Ishmael from a watery grave. The comparison of the bubble to a button is really unusual and, perhaps for that reason, significant. In colloquial usage, the word "button" is often used to signify the navel; the word also means the bud of a flower containing its seeds. Etymologically, "button" is derived from *bouter*, which means "to thrust upward."

The upward bursting of the "button-like bubble" clearly indicates the opening of a navel and the blooming of a flower. The creative upward thrust of life from the vital center of the sea is best explained in terms of life emerging out of the lotus-navel of Vishnu reclining on the floor of the primeval sea. As though to complete this suggestive imagery, Melville describes the sea as a "creamy pool." The sea on which Vishnu is believed to be reclining in his sleep of eternal wakefulness is a sea of milk, *khsirodadhi*, in Sanskrit.

The bursting of the button-like bubble also reminds us of

the "unscrewing of the navel," which has been explained in the mystic language of Hinduism as the death of the body and the liberation of the soul for eternal life. This is the unscrewing of the doubloon, a prize granted to Ahab and his crew, a disastrous death which opens the doorway to eternal life.

The image may be understood in the individual as well as the cosmic sense. Both of them signify the birth of a new life. The images of the doubloon, the navel, and finally the button are made most significant in the figure of the bubble, for the bubble so closely resembles the watery sac in which life evolves and bursts into birth out of the mother's womb.

The stormy sea has now changed to a creamy pool. The destructive force has been transformed into a creative impulse. One cycle of life has ended, making the beginning of a new one, known among the Hindus as *Yuga*. The beginning of a new cycle is marked by the suspension of evil. Melville is fully aware of this and describes it appropriately by saying: "The unharming sharks, they glided by as if with padlocks on their mouths; the savage sea-hawks sailed with sheathed beaks." The images of the vortex and the wheel supported by auxiliary images of the button-like bubble, the creamy pool, and others bring out clearly the Hindu concept of *Yuga*, an interminable cyclical movement of life rotating through eternity.

THE *RACHEL* SYMBOLIZES BOTH CHRISTIAN AND HINDU BELIEFS

This cyclical nature of life is indicated in another way. It is significant that Ishmael is picked up by a ship named Rachel. Earlier, a reference has been made to her lamentations for her missing children. Some Biblical scholars think of Rachel as representing "corporate motherhood," for she weeps for children she did not have and regards others' children as her own. In the Book of Matthew the story of Rachel's lamentation is associated with the slaying of the infants by Herod and the birth of Jesus Christ:

> In Ramah was there a voice heard, lamentation, and weeping, and great mourning, Rachel weeping for her children, and would not be comforted, because they are not.

Jesus was the only child that survived Herod's massacre of infants. Being in the same line of succession, Jesus may be regarded as the last son of Rachel. Rachel picking up the only surviving Ishmael is obviously suggestive of the birth of

Jesus Christ, or, at least, his survival in the total massacre of children by Herod. *Moby-Dick* begins with Christmas and may also be said to end appropriately with an event that suggests Christ's birth. Structurally the plot-movement of *Moby-Dick* is circular symbolizing the cosmic process of life which conforms to Hindu belief.

Moby Dick: Jonah's or Job's Whale?

Nathalia Wright

The two main biblical stories referred to in *Moby-Dick* are those of Jonah and Job. In the following essay, Nathalia Wright examines each story in order to determine which one Moby Dick is modeled after and show how it influences the thematics of the novel. Wright believes that Jonah's story suggests a moral universe with clear rules of cause and effect, while Job's story suggests an unknowable universe without any moral certainties. She concludes that *Moby-Dick* favors Job's story. Professor Wright taught literature at the University of Tennessee where she became an internationally recognized scholar in American literature. Her works include *Melville's Use of the Bible* and *American Novelists in Italy.*

That Melville made significant use in *Moby-Dick* of both the *Book of Jonah* (containing the most celebrated account of a whale in the Bible) and the *Book of Job* (the classic Hebrew presentation of the problem of evil in human experience) is obvious enough and has often been commented upon by critics. That he consistently represented the "leviathan" of Job as a whale, as it was in popular tradition though it had long been identified by biblical scholars as a crocodile, has been little more than noted, however, and never have his references to the sea monsters in these two biblical narratives been comparatively examined. Such an examination, interesting in itself, is rewarding for the answer it suggests to the central question of the novel: who or what is Moby Dick?

BOOK OF JONAH SUGGESTS A MORAL UNIVERSE

In the *Book of Jonah* the whale is an agent of Jehovah [the Hebrew name of God in the Old Testament], employed to coerce the prophet to obey the divine will by preaching to wicked

Nineveh [Assyrian city where Jonah was sent by God in biblical story to persuade inhabitants to end their evil ways]. This story is the subject of Father Mapple's sermon, which thus early in the novel—even before the *Pequod* puts to sea—presents the proposition that the universe is a moral creation, albeit one of constant conflict between good and evil.

Captain Ahab also adopts this point of view, though he differs radically from Father Mapple in identifying Moby Dick as an agent of an anti-Jehovah force. As Ishmael puts it in the chapter "Moby Dick"—the first of the two chapters devoted to defining the object of the novel's quest—Ahab sees Moby Dick not only as the creature which bit off his leg but as the "monomaniac incarnation of all those malicious agencies which some deep men feel eating in them," as "that intangible malignity which has been from the beginning; to whose dominion even the modern Christians ascribe one-half of the worlds; which the ancient Ophites of the east reverenced in their statue devil," as "all the subtle demonisms of life and thought," as, in short, "all evil." In feeling himself the innocent victim of an inscrutable supernatural power, however, Ahab invites comparison not with Jonah but with Job. The parallel is suggested by Ishmael at the conclusion of the same chapter: "Here, then, was this grey-headed, ungodly old man, chasing with curses a Job's whale round the world. . . ."

STORY OF JOB SUGGESTS AN AMORAL AND UNKNOWABLE UNIVERSE

Ishmael's own point of view, set forth in the next chapter, "The Whiteness of the Whale," is essentially unlike Father Mapple's, Ahab's, and that of the author of *Jonah*. Though he compares the fright produced in him by the spectacle of whiteness with "the instinct of the knowledge of the demonism in the world" which frightens the Vermont colt at the scent of a buffalo robe, Ishmael's explanation of his own feeling is that whiteness signifies absence of meaning and even non-existence. To him the White Whale is thus symbolic of a universe which, for all its marvels, is not only amoral but inscrutable—perhaps, indeed, a complete illusion. Excepting the last possibility, it is essentially the view of the universe expressed by the Hebrew Wisdom writers, most notably by the author of *Job*.

Indeed, Ishmael adopts that author's conception of the whale (as he took the "leviathan" to be), considered as a species, throughout the novel. The quotation in "Extracts" and Father Mapple's sermon aside, the story of Jonah and the whale is referred to only three times, each time face- tiously: when the barman in the whale-head-shaped bar at the Spouter-Inn is called Jonah and when in Chapters LXXXII and LXXXIII ("The Honor and Glory of Whaling" and "Jonah Historically Regarded") Jonah's experience is linked in mock heroic fashion with the feats of Perseus [in Greek mythology, the slayer of Medusa] and St. George [fourth- century Christian martyr who, legend claims, slayed a dragon] and the whole argument over its credibility is sati- rized. Ishmael's references to the sea monster in *Job* are, on the other hand, of serious import, and all convey the awe- some tone of the original description. That description com- prises Chapter XLI of *Job,* the last, climactic one of the four chapters devoted to Jehovah's reply to Job's complaints about his affliction, and pictures leviathan as uncontrollable by man and without moral value—as, indeed, the whole cre- ation is depicted in all these chapters.

There are six direct references to *Job* in *Moby-Dick,* all but one to Chapter XLI, three of them quotations. They occur in "Extracts," Chapters XXIV ("The Advocate"), XXXII ("Cetol- ogy"), XLI ("Moby Dick"), LXXXI ("The *Pequod* Meet the *Vir- gin*"), and in "Epilogue" (with its quotation from *Job* I, "And I only am escaped to tell thee"). In addition, the name of Captain Bildad may be considered an indirect reference, though as for the biblical Bildad, he, like Job's other two friends, takes the universe to be a moral one, in which good and evil acts are rewarded accordingly. In Chapter XXIV Job is said to have written "the first account of our Leviathan." In Chapters XXXII and LXXXI, Ishmael quotes from verses 4, 9, 7, and 26–29 of *Job* XLI, writing in the first, apropos of be- ginning his own account, "What am I that I should essay to hook the nose of this leviathan! The awful tauntings in Job might well appal me. 'Will he (the leviathan) make a covenant with thee? Behold the hope of him is vain!'" and in the second, apropos the sperm whale which is fast with three harpoons in him,

> In this the creature of whom it was once so triumphantly
> said—"Canst thou fill his skin with barbed irons? or his head
> with fish-spears? The sword of him that layeth at him cannot
> hold, the spear, the dart, nor the habergeon: he esteemeth iron
> as straw; the arrow cannot make him flee; darts are counted
> as stubble; he laugheth at the shaking of a spear!"

The reference in Chapter XLI, in which Ahab is said to be chasing "a Job's whale," is of particular interest, since it would seem to be Ishmael's most outspoken disagreement with his captain.

Above all, the cetological chapters of *Moby-Dick* may be considered the expression of Ishmael's *Job*-like point of view. These chapters—some forty-two in all or somewhat more than a third of the total hundred and thirty-five—begin with Chapter XXIV ("The Advocate") and end with Chapter CV ("Does the Whale Diminish?"). They have been both attacked as digressive, especially by early critics but also by twentieth-century ones, like John Freeman, and defended structurally as well as philosophically, notably by later critics like Newton Arvin and J.A. Ward. When they are taken as Ishmael's conception of the whale projected in biblical terms they have a significance hitherto unrecognized. They are to Ahab's pursuit of Moby Dick what Jehovah's reply is to Job's complaints: an oblique denial that morality is inherent in the creation. Like Jehovah, Ishmael bypasses the whole problem of evil in human experience, which obsesses both Job and Ahab, and describes a natural world which is neither good nor evil but sheerly marvelous, or in Job's words, "too wonderful for me." Even the tendency toward cannibalism which pervades this world appears thus, by no means the least marvelous aspect of it.

In relation to Ahab's fantastic speeches and actions in the course of his pursuit of Moby Dick, these chapters not only give a sane and factual account of whales and whaling, they imply that Ahab's view of Moby Dick is doubly false, that in the purely natural world no creature is good or evil and no ravener or ravened is guilty or innocent. Unlike Job, however, whose original sense of injustice he shares, Ahab is not brought to change his point of view by any new insight into this world, though his very profession offers him one.

The cetological chapters also represent a correction of Ishmael's own tendency to lose himself in abstract speculation about the nature of the universe and the identity of the self. As has often been pointed out, he is introduced as an outcast, is restored to the human community in consequence of shipping on the *Pequod,* and thus is appropriately the sole survivor of the wreck. His survival is also significant for another reason. The knowledge of cetology which he acquires seems calculated to save him from a fate similar to

Ahab's by persuading him of the purely physical nature albeit the endlessly marvelous complexity of the universe. Certainly the mood of wonder, exhilaration, even jocundity, pervading these chapters is in pointed contrast to the horror accompanying Ishmael's periods of metaphysical speculation and introspection. The source of the motto of the "Epilogue"—the words of Job's several servants who escaped to tell him of the catastrophes visited upon him—is thus singularly appropriate, since *Job* also is evidently the source of what comes to be Ishmael's prevailing world-view.

MOBY-DICK Favors Job's Whale

It should be pointed out, of course, that Melville himself did not wholly subscribe to Ishmael's or to *Job's* view of the universe. The shifting point of view in *Moby-Dick*, dominated as it is by the character of Ahab, is evidence enough, without looking at Melville's other works, from *Typee* to *Billy Budd*. As [nineteenth-century American novelist Nathaniel] Hawthorne wrote, after conversing with Melville in Liverpool in 1856:

> Melville . . . informed me that he had "pretty much made up his mind to be annihilated"; but still he does not seem to rest in that anticipation; and, I think, will never rest until he gets hold of a definite belief. . . . He can neither believe, nor be comfortable in his unbelief; and he is too honest and courageous not to try to do one or the other.

Or, as [twentieth-century English novelist] D.H. Lawrence put it, "Poor Melville! He was determined Paradise existed. So he was always in Purgatory. . . . He was born for Purgatory. Some souls are purgatorial by destiny."

In *Moby-Dick*, nevertheless, the argument seems resolved in favor of a physical rather than a metaphysical universe. Moby Dick is indeed "a Job's whale" rather than Jonah's. The sheer density of the cetological chapters is overwhelmingly persuasive. The unhuman universe in which Ishmael survives, floating on a calm sea past passive creatures of prey a day and night before being rescued, is finally distinguished, moreover, by a profound peacefulness—at least as profound as that of the metaphysical universe in *Billy Budd* on the morning of Budd's execution, when sky and air have first a luminousness and then a clarity of supernatural quality.

The Use of Folklore to Establish Humanism

Ray B. Browne

In this selection, Ray B. Browne argues that Melville uses folklore to create a philosophy of humanism, which emphasizes human concerns over divine expectations. Browne argues that the deliberate use of folklore and proverbs not only illuminates the novel's themes, but also reveals the characters to be classic archetypes. Seen in this universal context, the meaning of the characters and their relationship to the larger themes becomes clearer. Ray B. Browne is a Distinguished University Professor emeritus at Bowling Green State University and the author of over seventy books on literature and popular culture, including *Heroes and Humanities: Detective Fiction and Culture.*

In *Moby-Dick* Melville uses his folklore to establish a broader base and richer development for the book than would have been possible without it. Thus he provides at the same time more "truth" and more enjoyment. Most important, however, Melville's use of folklore, the blood-stream of humanity, deepens the roots of development for the triumph of humanism.

Melville's belief in the power of folklore is revealed in this work in two remarks. Always skeptical of everything but seldom dismissing out of hand anything that comments on the human situation, he questions: "Are you a believer in ghosts, my friend? There are other ghosts than the Cocklane one, and far deeper men than Doctor Johnson who believe in them." Later, Melville discusses how some Nantucketers distrust the story of Jonah, as "some skeptical Greeks and Romans . . . doubted the story of Hercules and the whale, and Arion and the dolphin; and yet their doubting those tra-

Ray B. Browne, *Melville's Drive to Humanism.* Lafayette, IN: Purdue University Studies, 1971. Copyright © 1971 by Purdue Research Foundation. Reproduced by permission.

ditions did not make those traditions one with the less fact, for all that."

FOLKLORE HELPS INTERPRET PAINTINGS

Melville begins working in folklore early in the book, at the Spouter-Inn, turning to folk wisdom to ground his authority on an appeal to highest authority. He is trying to fathom various and illusory meanings of the dark and greasy picture on the wall. He advances numerous theories and possible explanations as he demonstrates the complexity of truth, the "sublimity about it that fairly froze you to it." In the final analysis, however, Ishmael the naif, the innocent, the folk-figure, concludes that the symbol is clear. The drawing pictures a ship in a great hurricane with a whale impaling himself on the three mast-heads. The message is that nature and God in the whale descending from above are trying to destroy the ship of mankind but are unable to succeed. Ishmael makes clear that his interpretation is that of the folk: a final theory of his own, "partly based upon the aggregated opinions of many aged persons with whom I conversed upon the subject."

The wall opposite this picture is developed folkloristically also. On the wall are the weapons of white whalers, rusty, broken, and deformed. Their weapons, like white people's lives, are supported by myths and lies of one kind or another: "Some were storied weapons." One story is of Nathan Swain who "did kill fifteen whales between a sunrise and a sunset." Another story about a harpoon "so like a corkscrew now," shows the ubiquitousness of the whale, how he traveled from the Javan seas to the Cape of Blanco. This story is capped off by the belief that the iron traveled forty feet in the whale, from the tale to the head, like a restless needle sojourning in the body of a man.

PROVERBS ARE USED TO CLARIFY THEMES

Melville uses proverbs and folk-like proverbs freely to illustrate or prove a point. Sometimes they are integral, sometimes peripheral and comic. In examining the amazing character Queequeg and proving his superiority over other men, Melville discusses philosophers in general and the intuitive philosophy of Queequeg, rounding off his comment: "So soon as I hear that such a man gives himself out for a philosopher, I conclude that, like the dyspeptic old woman, he must have 'broken his digester.'" Later the mad prophet Elijah, talking with Ishmael and Queequeg, discounts the real need of a soul, by giving a proverb: "A soul's a sort of a fifth wheel to a wagon."

Proverbs are most widely used when the various sailors are in the forecastle at midnight before the squall. The setting itself is folkloristic. These sailors are nervous because they can sense the coming of the storm. The Long Island sailor reveals his nervousness in two good American proverbs: "Hoe corn when you may," and "all legs go to harvest soon." The Danish sailor attests to the seaworthiness of the ship in the storm with a proverb: "So long as thou crackest, thou holdest!" In the near-fight between Daggoo and the Spanish sailor, each combatant belittles the other with proverbs. Daggoo curses the Spaniard with "white skin, white liver!" to which the latter responds with "big frame, small spirit!" Even Ahab in his flight from all restraint against his coming battle with God in the whale cries out against Pip that there is too much in him that is cursing his malady—"like cures like." Then he clinches the proverb in his own repetition: "Oh! spite of million villains, this makes me a bigot in the fadeless fidelity of man!—and a black! and crazy!—but methinks like-cures-like applies to him too; he grows so sane again."

Less often Melville uses folk comparisons, similes, and metaphors to strengthen the fiber of his book. In describing the try-works, the terrifying open-mouthed flame, he says it "smells like the left wing of the day of judgment." In contrast, the product of that fire, the whale oil, is "as sweet as early grass butter in April."

FOLKLORE BUILDS CHARACTER

Folklore is used to build up character. Melville begins by saying that whalemen are as superstitious as other sailors, "unexempt from that ignorance and superstitiousness hereditary to all sailors." He continues: "No wonder then that ever gathering volume from the mere transit over the wildest watery spaces, the outblown rumors of the White Whale did in the end incorporate with themselves all manner of morbid hints, and half-formed foetal suggestions of supernatural agencies, which eventually invested Moby-Dick with new terrors unborrowed from anything that visibly appears." Melville then quotes both Olassen and Povelson about the terror of the sperm whale, and builds on their exaggerated statements: "yet in their full terribleness, even to the bloodthirsty item of Povelson, the superstitious belief in them is, in some vicissitudes of their vocation, revived in the minds of the hunters." "So that overawed by the rumors and portents concerning" Moby-Dick, many whalemen thought that the sperm whale could not be "hopefully pursued" by "mortal man," though some of the sailors "without superstitious accompaniments, were sufficiently hardy not to flee from the battle if offered." But one of the "wild suggestions" was that Moby-Dick was "ubiquitous," and "nor, credulous as such minds must have been, was this conceit altogether without some faint show of superstitious probability." One belief was that the whale had found the "nor' West Passage." This and other beliefs, "these fabulous narrations are almost fully equalled by the realities of the whalemen." Some whalemen went even further in their superstitions, "declaring Moby-Dick not only ubiquitous, but immortal. There was enough in the earthly make and incontestable character of the monster to strike the imagination with unwonted power."

The old Manxman—the oracle and shaman of the ship—engages in white voodoo or magic to tell when and under what conditions the whale will be encountered. In an obvious echo of *Macbeth*, he gives out information taught to him by the "old witch in Copenhagen" that, "If the White Whale be raised, it must be in a month and a day, when the sun stands in some one of these signs."

FOLKLORE HELPS DEFINE WHALE

Folklore is used to emphasize the whiteness of both the whale and the squid. Indicating the terribleness of the whale, Melville caps off his portrait with: "Nor even in our superstitions do we fail to throw the same snowy mantle round our phantoms; all ghosts rising in a milkwhite fog." According to legend and folklore few whale-ships ever beheld the white squid, and "returned to their ports to tell of it."

Twice folklore is used, both times with tongue-in-cheek frontier exaggeration, to describe the whale. "The Right Whale's head bears a rather inelegant resemblance to a gigantic galliot-toed shoe. Two hundred years ago an old Dutch voyager likened its shape to that of a shoemaker's last. And in this same last or shoe, that old woman of the nursery tale, with a swarming brood, might very comfortably be lodged, she and all her progeny." In describing the hare-lip of the right whale, Melville facetiously remarks, reaching to one of the most widespread folk beliefs about birthmarking, that "probably the mother during an important interval was sailing down the Peruvian coast, when earthquakes caused the beach to gape."

FOLKLORE IS USED TO REVEAL CHARACTERS

Folklore is also widely used in characterizing Ahab. Ahab is keenly aware of folk practices in dealing with sea weather. The proper way to "kill a squall, something as they burst a watersprout with a pistol" is to allow your ego full range and "fire your ship into it!" Folk analogy caps off Ahab's character delineation: "He lived in the world, as the last of the Grisley Bears lived in settled Missouri. And as when Spring and Summer had departed, that wild Logan of the woods, burying himself in the hollow of a tree, lived out the winter there, sucking his own paws; so, in his inclement, howling old age, Ahab's soul, shut up in the caved trunk of his body, there fed upon the sullen paws of its gloom!"

The poignancy of Ahab's Prometheanism [referring to Greek myth about Prometheus, who was punished for stealing fire from the gods and giving it to humans] is revealed folkloristically. In the powerful scene between himself and the carpenter, Ahab orders the carpenter to build a man, and especially to build another leg which when he mounts he "shall nevertheless feel another leg in the same identical place" where he should have his real leg. The carpenter replies "Truly sir, I begin to understand now. Yes, I have heard something curious on that score, sir: how that a dismasted man never entirely loses the feeling of his old spar, but it will be still pricking him at times. May I humbly ask if it be really so, sir?" To which Ahab, with great regret, responds, revealing the degree to which he has ceased being a mere man and has become in fact demonic: "It is, man. Look, put thy live leg here in the place where mine was; so, now, here is only one distinct leg to the eye, yet two to the soul. Where thou feelest tingling life; there, exactly there, there to a hair, do I."

FEDALLAH'S DEMONIC CHARACTER IS EMPHASIZED THROUGH FOLKLORE

The character of Fedallah and his eventual usurpation of Ahab's soul is boiled in the cauldron of witches' brew and demonism. From the moment he goes aboard the *Pequod* in Nantucket, we know that he is a devil. This picture is enlarged upon by superstitious Stubb and Flask after a right whale has been killed and made fast to the ship opposite the sperm whale. They remember that Fedallah who knows "all about ships' claims" has said that after the head of a sperm whale has been hoisted on the starboard and a right whale's on the larboard the ship can never afterwards capsize. Fedallah knows "all about ships' charms" because he is the devil. According to these two men, Fedallah coils his tail in his pocket or in the "eye of the rigging," and wears oakum stuffed in the toes of his boots. Ahab wanted him aboard so that like Faust and numerous other such dealers throughout folk history, he could make a bargain with him. Ahab makes the bargain, blending his soul with that of Fedallah in the famous scene where one shadow overmatches the other, and subsequently grows more and more demonic. When talking to the carpenter about building him another leg, Ahab touches on demonic creation, like Bannadonna later in "The Bell-Tower," by asserting that he will "get a crucible, and into it, and dissolve himself down to one small, compendious vertebrae." This flaming demonism grows stronger, when later Ahab brings to the blacksmith for his use in forging the magical harpoon the "nail-stubs of the steel shoes of racing horses," "the best and stubbornest stuff. . . Blacksmiths ever work," which will "weld together like glue from the melted bones of murderers."

The demonism increases in tempo and significance as the barbs for the harpoon are made magical through ritual. Ahab takes the characteristic oath: he will "neither shave, sup, nor pray," until the whale is destroyed. The points are then tempered in "pagan" blood drawn from "three punctures made in the heathen flesh," like the brew from [seventeenth-century English dramatist William Shakespeare's tragedy] *Macbeth*'s witches, all blessed—or cursed—with the demonic chant: "Ego non baptizo ten in nomine patris, sed in nomine diaboli!" ["I baptize you not in the name of the father, but in the name of the devil!"] "deliriously howled" by Ahab. These demoniac activities are further emphasized when Ahab gets false heaven's blessings in stretching the new towline until it "hummed like a harp-string," with which he bound pole and iron together "like the Three Fates." All ritual is capped off by the "wretched laugh" of Pip, the approval of a mad boy. Ahab grows as demon, drawing upon ritual, after the thunder has turned the needles of the compass. In correcting them, Ahab performs like a magician, or witch-doctor. He exercises his "subtle skill" in a manner to "revive the spirits of his crew." "Abashed glances of servile wonder were exchanged by the sailors, as this was said; and with fascinated eyes they awaited whatever magic might follow." Only Christian Starbuck fails to be mesmerized. By the time Moby-Dick is sighted, Ahab has become the devil as dog, one of the oldest and most popular forms for Satan. Probably drawing from "Ethan Brand" [a short story by nineteenth-century American novelist Nathaniel Hawthorne], Ahab sniffs out Moby-Dick like a "sagacious ship's dog."

Melville employs folklore in the form of omens to reveal the degree to which Ahab has gone insane. On the first day of the chase of the hated whale Starbuck uses the wrecked boat as an ill omen. Ahab rejects both the object as an omen and the idea of omens as such: "If the gods think to speak outright to man, they will honorably speak outright: not shake their heads and give an old wives' darkling hint." But the next day his madness has raged to the point where Ahab actually believes in omens, or uses them to sway the sailors to his evil purpose. After the boat has been wrecked a second time, Ahab rails: "Believe ye, men, in the things called omens? Then laugh aloud, and cry encore! For ere they drown, drowning things will twice rise to the surface; then rise again, to sink forevermore. So with Moby-Dick—two days he's floated—tomorrow will be the third."

The superiority of Queequeg over white men and their superstitions and religion is demonstrated through folklore. After the cannibal harpooner has been measured for his coffin, the Long Island sailor says: "Oh! poor fellow! he'll have to die now." But Queequeg, as though he were overturning such superstitions, gets well. It is Pip who cures him. While Queequeg is lying in his coffin, testing to be sure it is a comfortable place, Pip approaches and renders the last rites, in a minstrel parody of Christian practice. Starbuck, paraphrasing Shakespeare, builds on the situation by stating that he has heard that men in "violent fevers," "all ignorance have talked in ancient tongues," and have thus shown amazing wisdom. Pip reveals the depth of his wisdom in stating that Queequeg "dies game." "To all this ritual above and about him," the cannibal "lay with closed eyes, as if in a dream."

But though half dead while these Christian practices were being carried out, Queequeg rallied, saying that he could live or die as he willed. Melville's point is apparently that Queequeg here, as elsewhere, passes through Christian belief and practice in death and thereafter rose to a higher humanism. Thereafter he strove "in his rude way" to copy parts of the twisted tattooing on his body, the grotesque figures and drawings, onto the coffin, tying in this scene with the earlier one on "The Counterpane," in which Melville made it explicit that the heathenish symbols of the cannibal blend in indistinguishably with the symbols of Christian religion.

FOLKLORE INTENSIFIES AHAB'S DESTRUCTION

Finally, Melville employs folklore to heighten and intensify the drama of the final destruction of Ahab and his world. On the crucial third day (magic in both Christianity and folklore), as the captain sets out from the ship for the last time, he is twice-warned through folk wisdom of his impending doom. In the first place, the "first sharks that had been observed by the *Pequod* since the White Whale had been first descried," suddenly appear and, aware of their coming feast, follow Ahab's boat. "Whether it was that Ahab's crew were all such tiger-yellow barbarians, and therefore their flesh more musky to the senses of the sharks—a matter sometimes well known to affect them—however it was, they seemed to follow that one boat without molesting the others." In other words, as in folk belief that like cures like, sharks here are going to "cure" the shark-like devils on Ahab's boat.

Ahab, ever more aware of hovering disaster, experiences a phenomenon well established in folk belief—premonition of death through extra sensitivity: "Oh! my God! what is this that shoots through me, and leaves me so deadly calm, yet expectant,—fixed at the top of a shudder! Future things swim before me, as in empty outlines and skeletons."

This folklore is used just as richly and fully here as the popular theater was used. . . . In Melville more than in any other American writer folklore was accorded its great importance in the life of man.

CHAPTER 4

The Characters of *Moby-Dick*

READINGS ON
MOBY-DICK

Ahab's Inability to Understand the Whale Leads to His Self-Destruction

Charles H. Cook Jr.

Charles H. Cook Jr. reveals how Captain Ahab's insistence on seeing the whale only as evil causes his own death. Cook explores the various ways different characters view the whale, and how each viewpoint reflects their intractable vision of the universe and their place in it. Only Ishmael's vision of the whale, and therefore of the world, changes as he learns and matures, which is why he alone survives. Ahab, however, allows his own hatred of the world to dominate how he sees the whale, and the world, which leads to his self-destruction. Charles H. Cook Jr. is professor of English emeritus at Northeastern University.

In Chapter XLV of *Moby-Dick* appears Herman Melville's well-known admonition against scouting at the white whale as a fable or an allegory: "So ignorant are most landsmen of some of the plainest and most palpable wonders of the world, that without some hints touching the plain facts, historical and otherwise, of the fishery, they might scout at Moby Dick as a monstrous fable, or still worse and more detestable, a hideous and intolerable allegory." Although occasionally misinterpreted as a blanket condemnation of allegorical literature, this passage is for the most part rightly understood as Melville's (or Ishmael's) protest that white whales are realities, not imaginary sea-monsters. But scholars and critics have not yet exploited the possibility that this "intolerable allegory" statement may have much deeper significance. May it even be the key to the main theme of the novel and to the tragic flaw in Ahab's character? Aware of

Charles H. Cook Jr., "Ahab's 'Intolerable Allegory,'" *Boston University Studies in English*, vol. 1, Spring–Summer 1955, pp. 45–52.

the human temptation to project simple, personal meanings upon things which are formless or incomprehensible, Melville may be giving us the tragedy of a man who yields his whole soul to this temptation, who inflates his own private hurt into the hurt of all mankind, and who allegorizes the inflictor of this hurt as the dwelling place of all human evil. Is Ahab an example of that deadly brand of reformer whose obsession with one evil blinds him to the enigmatic ambiguity of the moral world? Is he the creator of a hideous and intolerable allegory?

Circumstances and facts favoring this interpretation of *Moby-Dick* are plentiful. Events in the main action of the story, the symbolism of the white whale, details of Ahab's character, and the numerous cetological digressions all support the idea. Moreover, this interpretation provides a defense for Melville against the frequent charge of vagueness. This apparent vagueness is actually an effect painstakingly cultivated by the author. By this means the reader is made to feel the baffling multiplicity and incomprehensibility of the universe which confronts the characters of the novel. The only character in *Moby-Dick* who succeeds in eliminating all vagueness from his mind is the monomaniacal Ahab. He discovers only a false and treacherous oneness focused upon the symbol of the white whale.

AHAB SEES THE WHALE AS EVIL

A quick review of the main story reveals the intolerable-allegory interpretation to be compatible with the main events of the plot. Ishmael, a man never entirely sure of anything but fairly respectful toward all possibilities, ships upon a whaler whose cosmopolitan crew cannot fail to suggest the varied races, nationalities, and classes of mankind. As the narrative voice of the author, Ishmael stands like a philosophical question mark, absorbing, experiencing, commenting, explaining, but always wondering and never imposing final meaning upon the enigmas that confront him. The other members of the crew have more definite but more limited personalities than Ishmael. Over them all reigns Ahab, obsessed, leading and driving his crew toward the habitat of Moby Dick, the ferocious white whale who has previously bitten off the captain's leg. But Ahab's original motive of personal revenge has already turned into something much more grand and weird. The whale has become, in Ahab's mind, an incarnation of the world's evil. Out of himself Ahab has projected upon the whale the evil inherent in mortality. By killing this monster he would bring mankind into the millennium. In his desperate pursuit, intent upon what he supposes to be the greatest boon to humanity, he surrenders human values and enlists the aid of evil in its own pursuit. He obtains his crew by deception, leading the members to believe that they are embarking on a regular whaling expedition to seek oil for the lamps of mankind. When the men comprehend the true purpose of the voyage and develop an obvious reluctance, Ahab leads them on by sheer power of will, by promises, and by trickery. Employing the mass-psychology of a [twentieth-century German dictator Adolf] Hitler and the scientific deception of a magician, he awes the men by converting a sailmaker's needle into a pointer for the ship's compass. At last he plunges to the depths of inhumanity when, for fear of losing the hot track of Moby Dick and consequently the chance of blasting evil from the world, he refuses to join the search for the lost sons of the captain of the *Rachel*. He refuses to respond to the exhortations of the golden rule. "Do to me as you would have me do to you in like case," pleads the *Rachel's* commander. "'Avast,' cried Ahab—'touch not a rope-yarn;' then in a voice that prolongingly moulded every word—'Captain Gardiner, I will not do it. Even now I lose time. Good bye, good bye.'" The outcome of this madness is the destruction by the angered whale of boat, crew, captain—all except Ishmael, whose survival is justified partly by the practical necessity of saving the narrator of the story but also by the questioning humility of his personality, which prevents him from committing Ahab's tragic error of allegorizing. To Ishmael the whale is doubtless a symbol, but a symbol of infinitely multiple significance beyond the full comprehension of any man. To Ahab, filled with monomaniacal egotism, the whale is an unmixed incarnation of evil and therefore, by Melville's standards, a hideous and intolerable allegory.

As the reader can see, the validation of this interpretation calls for evidence that the whale holds one kind of meaning for Melville and Ishmael and a different and more specific meaning for Ahab. Such evidence is abundantly and pointedly supplied within the novel.

First, Melville is eager that his readers should recognize the flesh-and-blood reality of creatures like Moby Dick—

whales whose unusual strength, appearance, and behavior have won them individual recognition. The point of the chapter entitled "The Affidavit," and in fact of most of the cetological material throughout the book, is that whales are not fictional or mythical creatures, but completely real. Evidence is desirable, Melville explains, to establish the "reasonableness of the whole story of the White Whale." Where wonders of the natural world are concerned, truth may require "as much bolstering as error." Without facts and statistics, "ignorant landsmen might scout at Moby Dick as a monstrous fable, or . . . a hideous and intolerable allegory." However, Melville is certainly not denying that the white whale has symbolic significance. Because of the vagueness of contemporary cetological information, and because of the many myths already associated with whales, Moby Dick provides an almost ideal symbol for the author's purposes.

THE CONTRADICTORY SYMBOLISM OF THE WHALE

Of what, then, is the whale a symbol? The novel provides a multitude of hints, but they are often contradictory. The author refuses to give his sanction to any one meaning. Ahab, to be sure, thinks that he has the whole enigma figured out, but his presumption is a major part of Melville's theme. Out of the tantalizing multiplicity of significances offered in the novel, the reader, like Ahab, can easily be misled into the error of choosing some specific *one.* To avoid this error, the reader should consider especially the chapter on "The Whiteness of the Whale." There it is made clear that whiteness, in various associations, can symbolize goodness, chastity, magnificence, supremacy, joy, innocence, religious purity, divinity, terror, ghastliness, ill omen, death, and the immense void of the universe. "And of all these things," Melville concludes, "the Albino Whale was the symbol. Wonder ye then at the fiery hunt?" The stress is upon no single meaning but upon the infinity of possibilities, upon man's bafflement in the face of that infinity. . . .

Because of their basic nature human beings experience overwhelming difficulty in their attempts to reconcile opposites or to contemplate opposing concepts simultaneously. To comprehend such opposites inter-extant in a single nature is almost beyond human capability.

> Anyone's experience will teach him that though he can take in an undiscriminating sweep of things at one glance, it is

quite impossible for him, attentively, and completely, to examine any two things—however large or however small—at one and the same instant of time; never mind if they lie side by side and touch each other. But if you now come to separate these two objects, and surround each with a circle of profound darkness; then, in order to see one of them, in such a manner as to bring your mind to bear on it, the other will be utterly excluded from your contemporary consciousness.

Man, then, has an essentially monistic nature. To attempt to interpret the whale in terms of the essentially monistic human intelligence is a dangerous business. But when the natural human monism becomes obsessive, it turns into monomania and the result is the tragic fate of Ahab.

Melville and Ishmael know only this of the white whale: it is a real and living part of our world, and its incomprehensibility lures man to seek in it some tremendous philosophical significance. Whether any such significance actually inheres in the whale is a question that Melville carefully avoids answering in any final form. Philosophical significance is chiefly a matter of human creativity. The meanings which most men find in the whale are actually in the beholders themselves. Even at best these meanings are apt to be monstrous oversimplifications of life. At worst they are madness. The white whale is (to quote the novel) "physiognomically a Sphinx," his brain "that geometrical circle which it is impossible to square," his head "an entire delusion.". . .

AHAB PROJECTS HIS OWN EVIL UPON THE WHALE

Captain Ahab commits the tragic error which Ishmael avoids. He converts this facelessness into an intolerable allegory. The evil which surges within his own heart is externalized and fastened upon the white whale, which is all-embracing and all-receiving in its incomprehensibility. Under the illusion that he has shoved the world's evil beyond arm's length, where it can be hacked out of existence without simultaneous expungement of the attacker himself, Ahab undertakes his mad venture.

> The White Whale swam before him as the monomaniac incarnation of all those malicious agencies which some deep men feel eating in them, till they are left living on with half a heart and half a lung. That intangible malignity which had been from the beginning; to whose dominion even the modern Christians ascribe one-half of the worlds; which the ancient Ophites of the east reverenced in their statue devil; —Ahab did not fall down and worship it like them; but

> deliriously transferring its idea to the abhorred White
> Whale, he pitted himself, all mutilated, against it. . . . All the
> subtle demonisms of life and thought; all evil, to crazy Ahab,
> were visibly personified, and made practically assailable in
> Moby Dick.

Ahab's error of allegorizing is partly the result of his having erred in a much more fundamental way. He has failed to
comprehend what Melville, along with [seventeenth-century
English poet John] Milton, held to be the basic truth of the
moral universe: that good and evil are inextricably involved
with one another in realms of mortality. As Milton pointed
out in [his 1644 essay] *Areopagitica*, and as Melville implies
by the ambiguous duality of his symbolism and by the tragic
outcome of *Moby-Dick*, any attempt to eradicate evil by ex-
ternal injunction or attack must, if it is pursued strongly, simultaneously eradicate the good which is involved with the
evil. Virtue, as Milton viewed it, constitutes a dynamic victory
of good over evil *within the individual soul*. When, in order to
externalize his own portion of evil, Ahab ignored the eternal
involvement of good and evil and made an allegory of the
white whale, he surrendered his own opportunity for virtue.
His degeneration is obvious and at last complete. He recruits
his whalers by deception, allies himself with evil, and in the
end flaunts the basic moral guide of humanity, the golden
rule. And, irony of ironies, he supposes that he is doing all
this *for* humanity, to rid the world of the very evil which he
enlists in the attack upon his own allegory of evil. When the
evil which Ahab envisions is finally blotted out, the means of
its extinction is not the death of the whale but the death of
Ahab himself. . . .

Possibly in the example of Ahab there lies a warning, un-
intentional on Melville's part. . . . Might the book even serve
as a warning for man in the twentieth century? Slightly
giddy with scientific success, a little blear-eyed from our
mad glimpse into the atomic nature of things, we presume a
capacity to see eventually into the heart of *all* things—even
to untangle, perhaps, the intricate knot of good and evil. In a
sense it is a noble presumption, as was Ahab's. But it is a
supremely dangerous one, for the rope has a way of tighten-
ing around the neck of the operator even as he is intent upon
loosening the strands of the main knot:

> Ahab's harpoon was darted; the stricken whale flew forward;
> with ignited velocity the line ran through the groove;—ran

foul. Ahab stooped to clear it; but the flying turn caught him round the neck, and voicelessly as Turkish mutes bowstring their victim, he was shot out of the boat, ere the crew knew he was gone. Next instant, the heavy eye-splice in the rope's final end flew out of the stark empty tub, knocked down an oarsman, and smiting the sea, disappeared in its depths.

The Heroism of Ahab

Alfred Kazin

Alfred Kazin argues that Captain Ahab's doomed quest for the white whale makes him not only tragic but also heroic. Ahab is heroic because he is willing to risk his life in order to seek the ultimate truth about humanity's place in the universe. However, because Melville's view is that the universe is indifferent to the plight of humanity, Ahab sacrifices all to prove what he wishes weren't true. Alfred Kazin edited the Riverside edition of *Moby-Dick* and is the author of *On Native Grounds: An Interpretation of Modern American Prose Literature.*

[*Moby-Dick*] is not only a great skin of language stretched to fit the world of man's philosophic wandering; it is also a world of moral tyranny and violent action, in which the principal actor is Ahab. With the entry of Ahab a harsh new rhythm enters the book, and from now on two rhythms—one reflective, the other forceful—alternate to show us the world in which man's thinking and man's doing each follows its own law. Ishmael's thought consciously extends itself to get behind the world of appearances; he wants to see and to understand everything. Ahab's drive is to *prove*, not to discover; the world that tortures Ishmael by its horrid vacancy has tempted Ahab into thinking that he can make it over. He seeks to dominate nature, to impose and to inflict his will on the outside world—whether it be the crew that must jump to his orders or the great white whale that is essentially indifferent to him. As Ishmael is all rumination, so Ahab is all will. Both are thinkers, the difference being that Ishmael thinks as a bystander, has identified his own state with man's utter unimportance in nature. Ahab, by contrast, actively seeks the whale in order to assert man's supremacy over what swims before him as "the monomaniac incarnation" of a superior power:

Alfred Kazin, *Contemporaries: From the 19th Century to the Present.* New York: Horizon Press, 1981. Copyright © 1981 by Horizon Press. Reproduced by permission of the Literary Estate of Alfred Kazin.

If man will strike, strike through the mask! How can the prisoner reach outside except by thrusting through the wall? To me, the white whale is that wall, shoved near to me. Sometimes I think there's naught beyond. But 'tis enough. He tasks me; he heaps me; I see in him outrageous strength, with an inscrutable malice sinewing it. That inscrutable thing is chiefly what I hate; and be the white whale agent, or be the white whale principal, I will wreak that hate upon him. Talk not to me of blasphemy, man; I'd strike the sun if it insulted me. For could the sun do that, then could I do the other; since there is ever a sort of fair play herein, jealousy presiding over all creations. But not my master, man, is even that fair play. Who's over me? Truth hath no confines.

AHAB'S ANGER AT AN INDIFFERENT UNIVERSE

This is Ahab's quest—and Ahab's magnificence. For in this speech Ahab expresses, more forcibly than Ishmael ever could, something of the impenitent anger against the universe that all of us can feel. Ahab may be a mad sea captain, a tyrant of the quarterdeck who disturbs the crew's sleep as he stomps along on his ivory leg. But this Ahab does indeed speak for all men, who, as Ishmael confesses in the frightening meditation on the whiteness of the whale, suspect that "though in many of its aspects this visible world seems formed in love, the invisible spheres were formed in fright." So man, watching the sea heaving around him, sees it as a mad steed that has lost its rider, and looking at his own image in the water, is tortured by the thought that man himself may be an accident, of no more importance in this vast oceanic emptiness than one of Ahab's rare tears dropped into the Pacific.

To the degree that we feel this futility in the face of a blind impersonal nature that "heeds us not," and storm madly, like Ahab, against the dread that there's "naught beyond"— to this extent all men may recognize Ahab's bitterness, his unrelentingness, his inability to rest in that uncertainty which, [twentieth-century psychoanalyst Sigmund] Freud has told us, modern man must learn to endure. Ahab figures in a symbolic fable; he is acting out thoughts which we all share. But Ahab, even more, is a hero; we cannot insist enough on that. Melville believed in the heroic and he specifically wanted to cast his hero on American lines— someone noble by nature, not by birth, who would have "not the dignity of kings and robes, but that abounding dignity which has no robed investiture." Ahab sinned against man and God, and, like his namesake in the Old Testament, becomes a "wicked king." But Ahab is not just a fanatic who leads the whole crew to their destruction; he is a hero of thought who is trying, by terrible force, to reassert man's place in nature. And it is the struggle that Ahab incarnates that makes him so magnificent a *voice*, thundering in Shakespearean rhetoric, storming at the gates of the inhuman, silent world. Ahab is trying to give man, in one awful, final assertion that his will *does* mean something, a feeling of relatedness with his world.

AHAB'S QUEST SYMBOLIZES HUMAN PASSION

Ahab's effort, then, is to reclaim something that man knows he has lost. Significantly, Ahab proves by the bitter struggle he has to wage that man is fighting in an unequal contest; by the end of the book Ahab abandons all his human ties and becomes a complete fanatic. But Melville has no doubt—nor should we!—that Ahab's quest is *humanly* understandable. And the quest itself supplies the book with its technical *raison d'être*. For it leads us through all the seas and around the whole world; it brings us past ships of every nation. Always it is Ahab's drive that makes up the *passion* of *Moby-Dick*, a passion that is revealed in the descriptive chapters on the whale, whale-fighting, whale-burning, on the whole gory and fascinating industrial process aboard ship that reduces the once proud whale to oil-brimming barrels in the hold. And this passion may be defined as a passion of longing, of hope, of striving: a passion that starts from the deepest loneliness that man can know. It is the great cry of man who feels himself exiled from his "birthright, the merry May-day gods of old," who looks for a new god "to enthrone . . . again in the now egotistical sky; in the now unhaunted hill." The cry is Ahab's—"Who's to doom, when the judge himself is dragged to the bar?"

Behind Ahab's cry is the fear that man's covenant with God has been broken, that there is no purpose to our existence. The *Pequod* is condemned by Ahab to sail up and down the world in search of—a symbol. But this search, mad as it seems to Starbuck the first mate, who is a Christian, nevertheless represents Ahab's real humanity. For the ancient covenant is never quite broken so long as man still thirsts for it. And because Ahab, as Melville intended him to, represents the aristocracy of intellect in our democracy, because he seeks to transcend the limitations that good conventional men like Starbuck, philistine materialists like Stubb, and unthinking fools like Flask want to impose on everybody else, Ahab speaks for the humanity that belongs to man's imaginative vision of himself.

THE PRACTICAL LIFE LEADS TO PHILOSOPHY

Yet with all this, we must not forget that Ahab's quest takes place, unceasingly, in a very practical world of whaling, as part of the barbaric and yet highly necessary struggle by man to support himself physically in nature. It is this that gives the book its primitive vitality, its burning authenticity. For *Moby-Dick*, it must be emphasized, is not simply a symbolic fable; nor, as we have already seen, can it possibly be construed as simply a "sea story." It is the story of agonizing thought in the midst of brutal action, of thought that questions every action, that annuls it from within, as it were—but that cannot, in this harsh world, relieve man of the fighting, skinning, burning, the backbreaking row to the whale, the flying harpoons, the rope that can take you off "voicelessly as Turkish mutes bowstring their victims." *Moby-Dick* is a representation of the passionate mind speaking, for its metaphysical concerns, out of the very midst of life. So, after the first lowering, Queequeg is shown sitting all night in a submerged boat, holding up a lantern like an "imbecile candle in the heart of that almighty forlornness . . . the sign and symbol of a man without hope, hopelessly holding up hope in the midst of despair." Melville insists that our thinking is *not* swallowed up by practical concerns, that man constantly searches for a reality equal to his inner life of thought—and it is his ability to show this in the midst of a brutal, dirty whaling voyage that makes *Moby-Dick* such an astonishing book. Just as Ahab is a hero, so *Moby-Dick* itself is a heroic book. What concerns Melville is not merely the heroism that gets expressed in physical action, but the heroism of thought itself as it rises above its seeming insignificance and proclaims, in the very teeth of a seemingly hostile and malevolent creation, that man's voice *is* heard for something against the watery waste and the deep, that man's thought has an echo in the universe.

Ishmael Represents Humanity's Tragic Plight

Bruce L. Grenberg

Bruce L. Grenberg's essay follows Ishamel's transition from a depressed, suicidal teacher on land to a happier, more fulfilled sole surviving sailor of the destroyed *Pequod*. Grenberg demonstrates how Ishmael's quest for meaning throughout the novel actually represents humanity's quest for meaning. He believes that it is only when Ishmael abandons his romantic notions of life and embraces a more realistic view of the world that he is able to become more self-realized. Bruce L. Grenberg retired in 1995 as associate professor of English at the University of British Columbia. He is the author of essays in *Chaucer Review, Modern Fiction Studies, Fitzgerald/Hemingway Review,* and elsewhere.

From the first page of *Moby-Dick* it is clear that the false starts, frustrations, and inevitable failures of Tommo, Omoo, Taji, Redburn, and White-Jacket have taken their toll on Melville's conception of the quest. In view of the diminishing worlds and constricting visions of Melville's first five novels, it is expressive of his resilient mind that he conceives one last and greatest quest for a whole vision of a whole world. But Melville was not one to leave any question unasked, and however desperate the conclusions to his first five novels, in *Moby-Dick* he manages to call up the energy for a sustained and comprehensive depiction of humanity's tragic plight.

Although Ishmael sets out on what proves to be a circumnavigating quest after the world's deepest and most fiercely kept secret, his motives and expectations in setting out are radically different from those of the hero-protagonists in the

Bruce L. Grenberg, *Some Other World to Find: Quest and Negation in the Works of Herman Melville.* Chicago: University of Illinois Press, 1989. Copyright © 1989 by the Board of Trustees of the University of Illinois. Reproduced by permission.

earlier fiction. Looking backward from *Moby-Dick*, we can perceive a perceptible if gradual change in Melville's conception of his questing heroes. The naive and apparently groundless belief in happy valleys, noble savages, and golden isles shared by Tommo, Omoo, and Taji had, as we have seen, dimmed greatly in Redburn and White-Jacket. But even Redburn has his deep-rooted memories of romantic glass ships and French coasts, and he holds before him always the prospect of recapturing his father's greatness—of returning from his enforced adventures to tell wonderful tales, over port, to admiring family and friends. And White-Jacket is sustained through all the miseries of the *Neversink's* cruise by the thought, however misplaced and ultimately denied, that he is homeward bound to the milk-and-honeyed land of liberty, fraternity, and equality. To Ishmael, as we shall see, these memories, these dreams and prospects are naught. From the first, his soul is all a "damp, drizzly November"; his going to sea is the last alternative of a desperate man—a "substitute for pistol and ball." And if, in the overview, the voyage of the *Pequod* is Melville's boldest quest in search of that "certain significance [that] lurks in all things," the utter wreck of its ending depicts with the emblematic simplicity of a parable Melville's horror at the fathomless and ineluctable mystery of the world's hard reality.

THE CAUSES OF ISHMAEL'S INTERNAL STRUGGLE

We don't have to read far to see somewhat into the causes of Ishmael's "hypos." First, he is no green youngster like Redburn, nor even so young a man as Tommo or White-Jacket, and he carries within him the accumulated frustrations and failures that characterize and define the life experiences of Melville's younger protagonists. Second, he is virtually penniless. He goes to sea as a sailor rather than as a passenger or a commodore because, he says whimsically, "they make a point of paying me for my trouble. . . . And there is all the difference in the world between paying and being paid." Behind the good humor of his explanation lies the hard truth of his life, that the world has yielded him the most meager sustenance, and that only grudgingly. His penniless state, however, is but a material sign of his deeper and more general alienation from life, and he is, to be sure, a proper Ishmael—an isolato and an outcast.

The opening pages of the novel define Ishmael's decision

to go to sea as the act of a desperate and outcast man, but when we read "The Counterpane," that strangely quiet, haunting chapter, we discover the true horror at the heart of Ishmael's life. The chapter begins quietly enough as Ishmael wakes about daylight in the Spouter-Inn, with Queequeg's arm thrown over him "in the most loving and affectionate manner." But the patchwork quilting of the counterpane, coupled with the "interminable Cretan labyrinth" of Quee-queg's tattooed arm, serves to carry Ishmael back to the mazed center of his own proper being. Ishmael's story of his childhood punishment is the most unguarded and unman-nered statement he makes about himself in the entire novel, and for that reason it is also the most revealing single state-ment we have of his true character.

The triggering cause of Ishmael's punishment is relatively insignificant, but the punishment itself, which was for him to be "packed . . . off to bed, though it was only two o'clock in the afternoon of the 21st June, the longest day in the year in our hemisphere," has stamped Ishmael for life. His expe-rience on that longest day of the year, one might say the longest day of his life, was so traumatic that he admits, even as he writes, that he "never could entirely settle" whether his experience was "a reality or a dream." Entombed in his "little room in the third floor," he is thrice removed from the light and life outside his prisoned self; he is the outcast wait-ing for the "resurrection" that never comes. Motherless to begin with, he is twice orphaned by a harsh and unforgiving stepmother. In the very midst of life he lies imprisoned, "the sun shining in at the window, and a great rattling of coaches in the streets, and the sound of gay voices all over the house."

All these things conspire to define the essential Ishmael—outcast among men. The essence of his nightmare lies in his waking to a room "wrapped in outer darkness" in which "nothing was to be seen, and nothing was to be heard; but a supernatural hand seemed placed in mine." The "nameless, unimaginable, silent form or phantom, to which the hand belonged" brings neither resurrection nor comfort to Ish-mael, however. A horrible inversion of the comforting mother Ishmael so longs for and cannot find, this nameless silent phantom serves as the very image of his pain and grief.

The horror of the young Ishmael's isolation and the greater horror of his being able only to imagine a comforting hand held out in darkness haunts the entire narrative. Indeed, for the narrator-Ishmael, all the terrors of the whale hunt and the catastrophe of the *Pequod*'s voyage do not compare to his early traumatic recognition that he is utterly alone in this world: "for several hours I lay there broad awake, *feeling a great deal worse than I have ever done since, even from the greatest subsequent misfortunes*" (my emphasis).

THE CONNECTION BETWEEN WHALING AND SUICIDE

Seeing Ishmael as we do at the beginning of his narrative—ageing, penniless, unwanted, and totally isolated in the world, it is perhaps surprising that he is willing to accept a substitute for pistol and ball. But in fact, the business of whaling is so linked in Ishmael's mind with image and portents of death that at times it seems not a substitute for suicide so much as a means of accomplishing it. Ishmael is no less quick than we are in making linked analogies between the larger world he inhabits and the Spouter-Inns and Peter Coffins of his immediate environment. New Bedford to him is a city of dreadful night; it is "Gomorrah" and "Tophet," lit only here and there by "a candle moving about in a tomb." He realizes, just as we do, that pondering the marble tablets in Father Mapple's Whaleman's Chapel is just another expression of his habit of "pausing before coffin warehouses, and bringing up the rear at every funeral" he meets.

In these opening chapters devoted to Ishmael's character there is a singularly fine distinction made between suicide and going whaling—between death and life; in Ishmael, Melville depicts a man who lives, yet has nothing to live for. Pondering the inscribed tablets of death in the Whaleman's Chapel, Ishmael sees in them the "deadly voids and unbidden infidelities . . . that seem to gnaw upon all Faith, and refuse resurrections to the beings who have placelessly perished without a grave"; yet he concludes, "Faith, like a jackal, feeds among the tombs, and even from these dead doubts she gathers her most vital hope." It is this faith born of despair that defines Ishmael's tenacious, yet tenuous hold upon life; thus he ends this chapter of tombstones and death with an affirmation: "three cheers for Nantucket; and come a stove boat and stove body when they will, for stave my soul, Jove himself cannot."

An unwanted child in an alien world, clinging to his fragile mortality, just as at the end of the voyage he will cling to Queequeg's life-buoy coffin, Ishmael not too surprisingly sees himself at the mercy of "the invisible police officer of the Fates." But his ruminations in "Loomings" on the Fates and the "grand programme of Providence," and his later philosophizing in "The Mat-Maker" on "chance, free will, and necessity," do more than define Ishmael's sense of powerlessness. They also define his all-important response to that powerlessness. Given the nature of Fate and Providence, Ishmael's general response is one of necessary acceptance, but more explicitly, Ishmael assumes for himself the role of inquisitor—looking into the "springs and motives" of the universe to uncover its fated, providential plan and, thereby, to discover himself.

ISHMAEL'S NEW REALISTIC ATTITUDE ABOUT THE WORLD

Unlike all Melville's earlier questing heroes, who sought a good, better, or even a best world, Ishmael perforce takes the world as it is and dives into it with a desperate curiosity. No Edenic valleys nor golden isles for Ishmael: only "the overwhelming idea of the great whale himself." With no new worlds to dream, Ishmael sets out for this world's "wild and distant seas," seeking out "the undeliverable, nameless perils of the whale," and "a thousand Patagonian sights and sounds." Accepting what he cannot change, Ishmael proposes for himself a limited hope, and even that is conditional upon the Fates: "I am quick to perceive a horror, and could still be social with it—would they let me—since it is but well to be on friendly terms with all the inmates of the place one lodges in."

All of Melville's romantic, questing heroes have been isolatoes, their dissatisfactions with conventional society leading them in search of other places, other times. But in *Moby-Dick*, Melville is unequivocal in revealing the certainties and the securities of conventional belief as illusions, the self-delusions of those who wilfully ignore the Patagonian sights and sounds of the world. Thus, in the opening chapters of the novel Ishmael is set apart from his fellow men, not by his condition, which all humanity shares, but by his heightened awareness of that condition. Ishmael confronts his destiny, while "crowds of water-gazers" merely stand, "fixed in ocean reveries." The unconscious compulsion that drives them to "get just as nigh the water as they possibly can without falling in" in Ishmael is carried to a higher pitch: he goes whaling.

Stubb and Starbuck Represent Moral Opposites

Kerry McSweeney

In the following essay, Kerry McSweeney contends that two of Ishmael's shipmates symbolize opposite moral positions that Ishmael must chose between. Second mate Stubb represents the common person, a brave, optimistic man who accepts the contradictions of life without examining them too closely. However, first mate Starbuck represents the Christian view of life, and as such questions the morality of their hunt for Moby Dick. Each position has certain strengths and weaknesses, which Ishmael must examine if he is to save himself. McSweeney is an English professor and the author of several critical works on nineteenth- and twentieth-century fiction and poetry.

Two of the mates on the *Pequod* figure importantly in *Moby-Dick:* Stubb, the second mate, and Starbuck, the first. Together with Flask, the third mate, they are introduced in chapters 26 and 27 not dramatically but through character sketches that contain in embryo almost everything that the reader needs to know or comes to learn about them. Each mate is shown to represent a different position on the intellectual and spiritual spectrum. Together with Pip they provide an important part of the background and the context for thinking about and assessing the positions occupied by Ahab and [Ishmael]. Flask is far and away the least interesting of the three, because he is almost totally unimaginative and unreflective. In the thumbnail sketch offered in chapter 27 he is said to be "so utterly lost . . . to all sense of reverence for the many marvels" of whales that he considers them "but a species of magnified mouse, or . . . water-rat." His unimaginativeness does not stand in the way of his occasionally providing lighter moments during the voyage, as in the description in chapter 34 of his discomfiture while at dinner at Ahab's cabin table. In chapter 81, however, his cruel pricking of the strangely discolored protuberance the size of a bushel on the flank of an old, blind whale is no laughing matter. It is rather an indication of his lack of reverence for whales in particular and of his "pervading mediocrity" (chap. 41) in general. The latter quality is further instanced in his unimaginative meditation on the doubloon—he wonders only about the number of cigars it will buy. And even at the moment of his death, the only significance he can find in the *Pequod's* fatal encounter with Moby Dick is also monetary—the comparatively "few coppers" that will come to his mother because of the premature termination of the voyage (chap. 135).

STUBB AS EVERYMAN

Stubb is a much more colorful and engaging character. In his introductory sketch in chapter 27 he is described as "a happy-go-lucky; neither craven nor valiant. . . . Good-humored, easy, and careless . . . an easy-going, unfearing man." Stubb presides over his whale boat "as if the most deadly encounter were but a dinner, and his crew all invited guests," and is as particular about the comfortable arrangement of his part of the boat "as an old stage-driver is about the snugness of his box." He handles his lance "as cooly and offhandedly as a whistling tinker his hammer," and even "hums old rigadig tunes" while at his perilous work. His most significant physical characteristic—indeed his visual leitmotiv [recurrent theme]—is his short black pipe, which is "one of the regular features of his face. You would as soon have expected him to turn out of his bunk without his nose as without his pipe." As with Dickens's humorous characters, Stubb is mainly brought to life through his distinctive speech, which is at its most flavorful and pungent in his exordia to his boat crew: "The devil fetch ye, ye ragamuffin rapscallions; ye are all asleep. Stop snoring, ye sleepers and pull. . . . Why in the name of gudgeons and ginger-cakes don't ye pull?" (chap. 48); "Start her, Tash, my boy—start her, all; but keep cool, keep cool—cucumbers is the word—easy, easy" (chap. 61); "Don't be afraid, my butter-boxes, ye'll be picked up presently—all right—I saw some sharks astern—St. Bernard's dogs, you know—relieve distressed travellers" (chap. 81).

In the long middle section of *Moby-Dick* a number of scenes in which Stubb dominates provide comic relief similar in its broad humor to that offered by Queequeg's encounters with civilized Christians in the early chapters of the book. Examples are found in the second mate's droll exchanges with Fleece the cook in "Stubb's Supper" (chap. 64) and in the account of how he duped the French captain in "The Pequod Meets the Rose-Bud" (chap. 91). But the more important and more interesting function of Stubb concerns the position he occupies in the spiritual and philosophical spectrum of *Moby-Dick.* Compared to Flask, Stubb does have some capacity to be moved by what is outside of himself. Since he can dream, as we know from "Queen Mab" (chap. 31), he can in his way respond imaginatively to events. He is also responsive enough to admire Ahab (chap. 118) and to be awed by the fire of the corposants (chap. 119). In the closing section of the book, he is sensitive enough to the mood of the *Pequod* to have a premonition of disaster and even to see a symbolic meaning in the lashing down of the ship's anchors (chap. 121). And if at the moment of his death his thoughts do not turn to speculative considerations (as do Ahab's and Starbuck's) at least he thinks of something more vital than money. As we know from his last words, Stubb goes to his watery death with the body of a young woman on his mind: "cherries! cherries! cherries! Oh, Flask, for one red cherry ere we die" (chap. 135).

STUBB'S BELIEF IN PREDESTINATION

Unlike Flask and Queequeg, Stubb even has enough inner life to be given a soliloquy or two through which his philosophy of life is directly presented to the reader. The most important of them is the first, which fills the one paragraph of "First Night-Watch" (chap. 39) and gives the second mate's reaction to "The Quarter-Deck" scene. "I've been thinking over it ever since, and that ha, ha's the final consequence. Why so? Because a laugh's the wisest, easiest answer to all that's queer; and come what will, one comfort's always left—that unfailing comfort is, it's all predestinated, . . . I know not all that may be coming, but be it what it will, I'll go to it laughing." This belief in supernatural causation—in events being predetermined by some force above and beyond man—might seem to move Stubb close to the position occupied by Ahab on the spiritual spectrum of *Moby-Dick.* His speech could even be thought a demotic rescoring of Ahab's oft-repeated belief in the immutable decrees of fate, the only difference being that in the prescripted drama in which they are acting, Ahab plays a tragic role and Stubb a comic one. One might further reflect that Stubb's part is more sympathetic than Ahab's in that it does not involve the rejection of what's kind to our mortalities, does not cut one off from others, and allows one to live neither suicidally nor solipsistically.

This is not the view of the matter that Ahab has, however, nor the view that the reader of *Moby-Dick* is invited to have. Both Ahab and Ishmael the narrator would agree with the Socratic dictum that the unexamined life is not worth living. Ahab's dismissive judgment of Stubb is that he is "brave as fearless fire (and as mechanical)" (chap. 133); and Ishmael earlier strikes a similar note in speaking of his "invulnerable jollity of indifference and recklessness" (chap. 41). Stubb is invulnerable and indifferent because he does not think. His belief that "it's all predestinated" is not the result of reflection, but a substitute for reflection—a pat formula that allows Stubb to be programmatically brave and metronomically cheerful. This is the reason psychological omniscience is never used in his presentation. In chapter 27, when he is first described to the reader, Ishmael remarks that "what he thought of death itself, there is no telling." There is no telling not because Ishmael's narratorial powers fail him when he comes to the *Pequod*'s second mate, but because there is nothing to tell. Stubb has no inner life. As we have seen, he can in his way respond imaginatively to natural facts but never to the extent that he is teased into thought and speculation.

STARBUCK AS CHRISTIAN

While it is hard not to agree with Ahab's scornful dismissal of Stubb's mechanical nature, it is more difficult, at least initially, to agree with his insistence that the second mate and the first are opposite equals: that "Starbuck is Stubb reversed, and Stubb is Starbuck; and ye two are all mankind" (chap. 133). Starbuck is, after Ahab and Ishmael, the most important character in *Moby-Dick* and the richest characterization in terms of both psychological depth and thematic implication. The most important single fact about Starbuck is that he is a Christian. . . .

Starbuck is the exemplary Christian in *Moby-Dick*. He is first mentioned at the end of chapter 21 when a shipmate observes in passing that the first mate is a "good man, and a pious." The accuracy of this remark is confirmed in the character sketch offered in chapter 26 that uses psychological omniscience to probe the depths of Starbuck's inner life. A "staid, steadfast man" with a basic ruggedness in his nature, Starbuck possesses courage that is not the devil-may-care fearlessness of Stubb but a useful and practical commodity, one of "the great staple outfits of the ship, like her beef and her bread, and not to be foolishly wasted." Yet for all his "hardy sobriety and fortitude" Starbuck is for a seaman "unusually conscientious and [has] a deep natural reverence." It is not unusual that he is superstitious; what is out of the ordinary is that the "outward portents and inward presentiments" that are his seem "rather to spring, somehow, from intelligence than from ignorance." The "welded iron of his soul" is still further bent by "his faraway domestic memories of his young Cape wife and child" and his "terrible . . . remembrances" of the loss at sea of his own father and brother.

Ishmael's immediate purpose in pointing up these humane, softening qualities of Starbuck's nature is to explain at the outset how a man of such a strong character will so easily become subservient to Ahab's dark power. The key point is that Starbuck's courage is more a physical than a metaphysical quality; it "cannot withstand those more terrific, because more spiritual terrors, which sometimes menace you from the concentrating brow of an enraged and mighty man." The reason he cannot stand up to Ahab is not that Starbuck lacks the capacity for spiritual perception (as does Stubb, for example, who is similarly cowed). It is rather that Starbuck's vision is too land-based, too rooted in natural and domestic pieties and insufficiently tempered by exposure not to the physical but to the metaphysical perils of the ocean. To recall an image used elsewhere in *Moby-Dick,* Starbuck, unlike Ahab, has not pushed off from the green and insular Tahiti within and encountered the terrors of the half-known life.

STARBUCK'S MORALITY SUCCUMBS TO AHAB'S INFLUENCE

The moment of "the fall of valor in the soul" of Starbuck, predicted in chapter 27, occurs in the quarterdeck scene in chapter 36. It is Ahab who remarks the moment. Starbuck has instinctively cried out that the captain's plan to wreak "vengeance on a dumb brute" seems blasphemous. But like the rest of the crew he is silenced by Ahab's demonstration of his powers of spiritual perception in his speech about visible objects being merely pasteboard masks. This speech ends with an aside in which Ahab notes that Starbuck has now become contaminated, and consequently incapacitated, by his own more powerful vision: "Something shot from my dilated nostrils, he has inhaled it in his lungs. Starbuck now is mine." The next person to speak in the scene is Starbuck, who murmurs lowly, "God keep me!—keep us all!"

In his soliloquy in chapter 38 ("Dusk") Starbuck struggles to understand what has happened to him on the quarterdeck. "My soul is more than matched," he reflects, "she's overmanned; and by a madman! . . . He drilled deep down, and blasted all my reason out of me! I think I see his impious end, but feel that I must help him to it." Starbuck goes on to console himself with the Christian hope that God may choose to thwart Ahab's blasphemous plan: "His heaven-insulting purpose, God may wedge aside." And at the end of his meditation the first mate again hitches his wagon to a Christian star: "Oh, life! 'tis in an hour like this, with soul beat down and held to knowledge,—as wild, untutored things are forced to feed—Oh, life! 'tis now that I do feel the latent horror in thee! but 'tis not me! that horror's out of me! and with the soft feeling of the human in me, yet will I try to fight ye, ye grim, phantom futures! Stand by me, hold me, bind me, O ye blessed influences!" This passage deserves close attention. In it Starbuck seems poised on the brink of recognition of the "latent horror" of life, and ready to begin the passage from earthly felicities to heart-woes, from the insular Tahiti to the terrors of the half-known life, from all that's kind to our mortalities to the howling infinite. But at the last psychological moment, so to speak, Starbuck pulls back from this knowledge and denies that the horror of life has any essential connection with him: "that horror's out of me!" he insists. What Starbuck refuses to recognize is that the line between land and sea, blessed and blasphemous, loveliness and horror, does not run between humanity and nature or between people, but rather runs through each individual. Starbuck prefers to remain cocooned in "the soft feeling of the human in me" and since (as he himself recognizes) such softness can hardly prevail against "ye grim, phantom futures" he is forced to put his trust in a supernatural softness, in "ye blessed influences" above. Such a posture may be a version of Christian submissiveness to the will of God; but it is also an example of self-willed spiritual immaturity, of remaining a provincial and a sentimentalist in Truth.

Starbuck appears only intermittently and never for very long in the middle section of *Moby-Dick,* and when he does he is always in character. In chapter 41 the narrator sums up what the reader has already been both told and shown: that the crew of the *Pequod* is "morally enfeebled . . . by the incompetence of mere unaided virtue or right-mindedness in Starbuck." The first mate is predictably appalled by the "white ghost" of the giant squid in chapter 59; and in chapter 99, as we have seen, he furnishes a Christian interpretation of what is depicted on the doubloon. Starbuck's interpretation of Pip's madness in chapter 110 also shows his habitual desire to find a soft, supernatural meaning in natural facts. "So to my fond faith," he avers, "poor Pip, in this strange sweetness of his lunacy, brings heavenly vouchers of all our heavenly homes." Needless to say, this is hardly as penetrating or convincing an analysis as that supplied by Ishmael the narrator. Starbuck's symbolic perceptions in chapter 114 ("The Gilder") similarly point up his naive refusal to face the spiritual facts. Ahab's gazing out on the blessed calm of an exceptionally lovely day leads to his profound meditation on "the secret of our paternity." The same scene prompts in Starbuck's reverie only another example of his self-inflicted spiritual blindness, his refusal to acknowledge the horror in life. "Loveliness unfathomable," he says as he looks down at the surface of the golden sea, "Tell me not of thy teeth-tiered sharks, and thy kidnapping cannibal ways. Let faith oust fact: let fancy oust memory; I look deep down and do believe."

Starbuck's moral enfeeblement is again instanced in chapter 123 ("The Musket") in his agonized self-debate over whether to kill Ahab. And his soft human qualities are again instanced in the scene with Ahab in "The Symphony" (chap. 132). On the third day of the chase in chapter 135—the day of his death—Starbuck is at his most sympathetically moving as he describes his strange sense that his life's journey is coming to an end. "Future things swim before me, as in empty outlines and skeletons; all the past is somehow grown dim. Mary, girl! thou fadest in pale glories behind me; boy! I seem to see but thine eyes grown wondrous blue." At the climactic moment, Starbuck resolves to die like a man fighting to the last and seems momentarily to doubt the efficacy of his Christian beliefs: "Is this the end of all of my bursting prayers? all my life-long fidelities? . . . My God, stand by me now!" The answer is that yes, this is the end. In the Christian hymn sung by the congregation of the Whaleman's Chapel in chapter 9, the castaway, arched over by the ribs and terrors of the whale and plunging to despair, calls on his God, and is rescued from his black distress. But there is no such "Deliverer God" for Starbuck. And while there is much for the tender-minded to be moved by in his pathetic end, the tough-minded reader will recognize the truth of Ahab's remark about the similarity of Starbuck and Stubb. The difference between the latter's "ha" and the former's Christian God is one of degree only, not of kind. Both notions of a supernatural final consequence serve to release their believers from the burden of encountering, recognizing, and accepting into consciousness what the older Ishmael calls the knowledge of the demonism of the world. This is a burden that the older Ishmael and Ahab both carry.

Father Mapple as Moral Prophet

Howard P. Vincent

Howard P. Vincent analyzes Father Mapple's sermon and how it emphasizes the central theme of resurrection through renunciation of the prideful self and the embracing of the divine self. Vincent further argues that because each of the main characters corresponds to some aspect of Jonah's story, Mapple's sermon prophesies the fates of these characters.

Vincent, a world-renowned Melville scholar, is the editor of a collection of Melville's poems and the author of many other critical works, including *Daumier and His World*.

Melville undoubtedly intended that Father Mapple's sermon should be the vehicle for the central theme of *Moby-Dick*. . . . Philosophically, *Moby-Dick* remains closed to us until we understand Father Mapple's sermon on Jonah and the Whale. With this key Melville unlocked his novel.

The sermon is a skillful adaptation of the Old Testament book of Jonah, especially that part dealing with Jonah's nautical adventures. The sonorous Biblical rhythms may be distinctly heard in Mapple's words. Diction and imagery suit well the old whaleman-preacher and a whaling audience. The setting of the sermon strengthens its message: the central theme first foreshadowed by the physical isolation of the minister from his flock:

> No, thought I, there must be some sober reason for this thing; furthermore, it must symbolize something unseen. Can it be, then, that by that act of physical isolation, he signifies his spiritual withdrawal for the time, from all outward worldly ties and connexions? Yes, for replenished with the meat and wine of the word, to the faithful man of God, this pulpit, I see, is a self-containing stronghold—a lofty Ehrenbreitstein, with a perennial well of water within the walls.

Howard P. Vincent, *The Trying-Out of* Moby-Dick. Boston: Houghton Mifflin, 1949.

Melville explains that Father Mapple's climb up the rope ladder to his pulpit is not a "trick of the stage." The reader sees it as a symbolical act similar in vein to the symbolical gestures and motions of [nineteenth-century American novelist] Nathaniel Hawthorne's characters—for instance, in "The Minister's Black Veil." Part of the nautical atmosphere of *Moby-Dick*, the isolating prow pulpit symbolizes the fundamental isolation of all men—a point underscored in the account of the waiting audience: "Each silent worshipper seemed purposely sitting apart from the other, as if each silent grief were insular and incommunicable." Everyman is an island—an isolato, Melville later says—and in nothing is he more alone than in his relation to his God. Such is Melville's implication.

MAPPLE JUSTIFIES THE WAYS OF GOD

No less than [seventeenth-century English poet] John Milton, Father Mapple seeks in his sermon to justify the ways of God to man. The relationship of the individual soul to God is difficult to determine and demands a consideration of the nature of "self" and selfhood. And as has been argued in discussing the opening line, "Call me Ishmael," *Moby-Dick* is concerned with the problem of self-realization. Melville attempts in Father Mapple's sermon to establish the profoundest meaning of the concept of "self." Self is made up of many selves; what we call self is a unification of various selves, as the political, the economic, the biological, the professional, the racial. Like all other phenomena, Selfhood resolves itself into the eternal dialectic of the One and the Many. Father Mapple's sermon is a device, a touchstone for testing the revelations of selfhood made in Ahab, Queequeg, or Starbuck— all variously inadequate or superficial when compared with the wisdom of Mapple's definition. The individualism of Father Mapple is Christian, insisting that the personal will must submit to the will of God, personal self must be submerged in the Divine self. Father Mapple's sermon is built on the theme most memorably stated by [fourteenth-century Italian poet] Dante [Alighieri]: "In His will is our peace." Father Mapple establishes in whaling language and through a whaling story the Christian paradox that the fullest selfhood may be won only by the annihilation of self.

Father Mapple tells his audience that the story of Jonah is a "two-stranded" lesson: the first strand a story of sin, punishment, and repentance; the second strand the account of Jonah's deliberate defiance of God's will. Mapple drives his point home: "And if we obey God we must disobey ourselves; and it is in this disobeying ourselves, wherein the hardness of obeying God consists." As the story of *Moby-Dick* unfolds, we realize the relevance, thematically as well as wittily, of the sermon on Jonah, for soon Jonah's fugue is repeated in the flight of Ahab. Ahab will set out on his vengeful voyage, determined to assert his might against the White Whale, and in defiance of the desires of his crew. But whereas Jonah at last heeded the will of God in time to save the ship and to still the storm, Ahab, unrepentant, imposes his will upon his men so that both he and the *Pequod* crew are destroyed. Ahab's defiance of the storm in "The Candles" is in ironic contrast to Jonah's repentance; in Father Mapple's sermon we behold a man saved by a whale, but in Ahab's act we see a man destroyed by one. Humility and submission are the sign of Father Mapple's "self"; pride and arrogant confidence the sign of Ahab's.

JONAH'S STORY INTRODUCES THE THEME OF RESURRECTION THROUGH RENUNCIATION

Melville, in Father Mapple's message, does not neglect the meaning of the three days Jonah spent within the whale's belly, singing his canticle to Jehovah. Though the words of Jesus, "Even as Jonah descended into the belly of the whale for three days and three nights, even so shall the Son of God descend into the tomb and rise again," are not quoted, it is clear from the language of the sermon that Melville had seen Jonah's experience as a form of resurrection. The correlation is rather clear:

> As we have seen, God came upon him in the whale, and swallowed him down to living gulfs of doom, and with swift slantings tore him along "into the midst of the seas," where the eddying depths sucked him ten thousand fathoms down, and "the weeds were wrapped about his head," and all the watery world of woe bowled over him. Yet even then beyond the reach of any plummet—"out of the belly of hell"—when the whale grounded upon the ocean's utmost bones, even then, God heard the engulphed, repenting prophet when he cried. The God spake unto the fish; and from the shuddering cold and blackness of the sea, the whale came breaching up towards the warm and pleasant sun, and all the delights of air and earth; and "vomited out Jonah upon the dry land"; when the word of the Lord came a second time; and Jonah, bruised

and beaten—his ears, like two sea-shells, still multitudi-
nously murmuring of the ocean—Jonah did the Almighty's
bidding. And what was that, shipmates? To preach the Truth
to the face of Falsehood! That was it!

The graphic and poetic power of such phrases as "the ocean's
utmost bones," or the delicate, yet strong, manipulation of an-
titheses such as "shuddering blackness of the sea" and "the
warm and pleasant sun"; the skillful planting of the word
"delight" which will be picked up again in the closing words
of the sermon; and the melodic felicity of "still multitudi-
nously murmuring of the sea" or "the engulphed, repenting
prophet"—all this should not distract us from examining the
symbolical significance of Father Mapple's paragraph. . . .
Melville's passages in . . . *Moby-Dick* set forth symbols of
death and rebirth. To be born again, psychologically and re-
ligiously, is to renounce an old self so as to assume a new self,
a new and deeper principle of life. [Nineteenth-century English poet John] Keats described the process as "dying into
life." Stated most profoundly, as by Melville through Father
Mapple, it is to renounce personal desire, and to accept the
will of God.

Father Mapple closes his sermon with an unambiguous
declaration of his point: to be reborn one must forget self in
the service of God—thus, and only thus, may happiness (Delight) be found, the truest selfhood attained:

> Delight is to him—a far, far upward, and inward delight—
> who against the proud gods and commodores of this earth,
> ever stands forth his own inexorable self. Delight is to him
> whose strong arms yet support him, when the ship of this
> base treacherous world has gone down beneath him. Delight
> is to him, who gives no quarter in the truth, and kills, burns,
> and destroys all sin though he pluck it out from under the
> robes of Senators and Judges. Delight,—top-gallant delight is
> to him, who acknowledges no law or lord, but the Lord his
> God, and is only a patriot to heaven. Delight is to him, whom
> all the waves of the billows of the seas of the boisterous mob
> can never shake from this sure Keel of the Ages. And eternal
> delight and deliciousness will be his, who coming to lay him
> down, can say with his final breath—O Father!—chiefly
> known to me by Thy rod—mortal or immortal, here I die. I
> have striven to be Thine, more than to be this world's, or
> mine own. Yet this is nothing; I leave eternity to Thee; for
> what is man that he should live out the lifetime of his God?

Delight is to him who reads Father Mapple's peroration. English prose is nowhere superior. The upward thrust of these

climactic sentences through the relentless repetition of "delight," the bold use of alliteration in the stabbing dentals, and the unexpectedness and perfection of the adjective "eternal" placed before the final "delight"—these and other effects (allusion, cadences) are the exercise of one both craftsman and artist.

No less powerful is the passage in its statement of spiritual truth, or in its enunciation of the dominant theme of *Moby-Dick*. In its recognition of the place of regeneration in spiritual maturation, and in its understanding of the deepest meaning of selfhood, Father Mapple's sermon is a far cry from the talk of selfhood heard from other Americans of Melville's day: [nineteenth-century American philosopher and poet Ralph Waldo] Emerson or [nineteenth-century American poet Walt] Whitman. The young Emerson who lay on his bed dreaming pleasantly of the harmony of God's world is not in the same church with Melville, whose appreciation of the terror and evil of life (learned on the pulses and not from texts) seems much more consonant with the harsh facts of common human experience.

From his eloquent and passionate affirmation the rest of *Moby-Dick* unfolds. Ahab no less than Father Mapple is in search of an Absolute, be its name God or Moby Dick, but unlike the whaleman-preacher, Ahab acknowledges no law but his own; his search will be carried on in self-assertion, not in self-submission. In the early, unrepentant Jonah, Ahab has been prefigured. Ahab defies God; his *hybris* [in Greek tragedy excessive pride toward gods] is the antithesis of Jonah's submission. Great as Ahab is, he is not, to borrow a phrase from Keats, "magnanimous enough to annihilate self." Striving to be God himself, or in worshiping false gods (even as the Ahab of the Old Testament worshiped Baal), Ahab will never know delight. "Delight," Father Mapple states significantly and memorably, "can only be to him who has striven to be God's." Not to him who strives to be God. Ahab should have been one of the silent worshipers at the Seaman's Bethel.

CHAPTER 5

The Reflection of American Society in *Moby-Dick*

READINGS ON
MOBY-DICK

The Doomed Voyage of America's White Society

D.H. Lawrence

D.H. Lawrence argues that *Moby-Dick* is symbolic of the inevitable demise of the dominance of white society in America. To Lawrence, the quest for the white whale represents America's quest to maintain the Caucasian ruling class. It is inevitable that in seeking such an unworthy goal, the ship should be sunk. The novel then becomes a cautionary tale, warning Americans to change their course or be doomed. English novelist D.H. Lawrence (1885–1930) is the author of the acclaimed novels *Sons and Lovers* and *Women in Love*.

Moby Dick, *or the White Whale*.

A hunt. The last great hunt.

For what?

For Moby Dick, the huge white sperm whale: who is old, hoary, monstrous, and swims alone; who is unspeakably terrible in his wrath, having so often been attacked; and snow-white.

Of course he is a symbol.

Of what?

I doubt if even Melville knew exactly. . . .

It is a great book.

At first you are put off by the style. It reads like journalism. It seems spurious [not genuine]. You feel Melville is trying to put something over you. It won't do.

And Melville really is a bit sententious [fond of pompous moralizing]: aware of himself, self-conscious, putting something over even himself. But then it's not easy to get into the swing of a piece of deep mysticism when you just set out with a story.

Nobody can be more clownish, more clumsy and senten-

D.H. Lawrence, *Studies in Classic American Literature*. New York: The Viking Press, 1971.

tiously in bad taste, than Herman Melville, even in a great book like *Moby Dick.* He preaches and holds forth because he's not sure of himself. And he holds forth, often, so amateurishly. . . .

MELVILLE REFLECTS EMOTIONAL ISOLATION OF AMERICANS

But he was a deep, great artist, even if he was rather a sententious man. He was a real American in that he always felt his audience in front of him. But when he ceases to be American, when he forgets all audience, and gives us his sheer apprehension of the world, then he is wonderful, his book commands a stillness in the soul, an awe.

In his "human" self, Melville is almost dead. That is, he hardly reacts to human contacts any more; or only ideally: or just for a moment. His human-emotional self is almost played out. He is abstract, self-analytical and abstracted. And he is more spell-bound by the strange slidings and collidings of Matter than by the things men do. In this he is like [nineteenth-century American writer Richard Henry] Dana. It is the material elements he really has to do with. His drama is with them. He was a futurist long before futurism found paint. The sheer naked slidings of the elements. And the human soul experiencing it all. So often, it is almost over the border: psychiatry. Almost spurious. Yet so great.

It is the same old thing as in all Americans. They keep their old-fashioned ideal frock-coat on, and an old-fashioned silk hat, while they do the most impossible things. There you are: you see Melville hugged in bed by a huge tattooed South Sea Islander, and solemnly offering burnt offering to this savage's little idol, and his ideal frock-coat just hides his shirt-tails and prevents us from seeing his bare posterior as he salaams, while his ethical silk hat sits correctly over his brow the while. That is so typically American: doing the most impossible things without taking off their spiritual get-up. Their ideals are like armour which has rusted in, and will never more come off. And meanwhile in Melville his bodily knowledge moves naked, a living quick among the stark elements. For with sheer physical vibrational sensitiveness, like a marvellous wireless-station, he registers the effects of the outer world. And he records also, almost beyond pain or pleasure, the extreme transitions of the isolated, far-driven soul, the soul which is now alone, without any real human contact.

The first days in New Bedford introduce the only human being who really enters into the book, namely, Ishmael, the "I" of the book. And then the moment's heart's-brother, Queequeg, the tattooed, powerful South Sea harpooner, whom Melville loves as Dana loves "Hope". The advent of Ishmael's bedmate is amusing and unforgettable. But later the two swear "marriage", in the language of the savages. For Queequeg has opened again the flood-gates of love and human connexion in Ishmael.

"As I sat there in that now lonely room, the fire burning low, in that mild stage when, after its first intensity has warmed the air, it then only glows to be looked at; the evening shades and phantoms gathering round the casements, and peering in upon us silent, solitary twain: I began to be sensible of strange feelings. I felt a melting in me. No more my splintered heart and maddened hand were turned against the wolfish world. This soothing savage had redeemed it. There he sat, his very indifference speaking a nature in which there lurked no civilized hypocrisies and bland deceits. Wild he was; a very sight of sights to see; yet I began to feel myself mysteriously drawn towards him."—So they smoked together, and are clasped in each other's arms. The friendship is finally sealed when Ishmael offers sacrifice to Queequeg's little idol, Gogo.

"I was a good Christian, born and bred in the bosom of the infallible Presbyterian Church. How then could I unite with the idolater in worshipping his piece of wood? But what is worship?—to do the will of God—*that* is worship. And what is the will of God?—to do to my fellow man what I would have my fellow man do to me—*that* is the will of God."— Which sounds like [American statesman] Benjamin Franklin [1706–1790], and is hopelessly bad theology. But it is real American logic. "Now Queequeg is my fellow man. And what do I wish that this Queequeg would do to me? Why, unite with me in my particular Presbyterian form of worship. Consequently, I must unite with him; ergo, I must turn idolater. So I kindled the shavings; helped prop up the innocent little idol; offered him burnt biscuit with Queequeg; salaamed before him twice or thrice; kissed his nose; and that done, we undressed and went to bed, at peace with our own consciences and all the world. But we did not go to sleep without some little chat. How it is I know not; but there is no place like bed for confidential disclosures between friends.

Man and wife, they say, open the very bottom of their souls to each other; and some old couples often lie and chat over old times till nearly morning. Thus, then, lay I and Queequeg—a cosy, loving pair——"

You would think this relation with Queequeg meant something to Ishmael. But no. Queequeg is forgotten like yesterday's newspaper. Human things are only momentary excitements or amusements to the American Ishmael. Ishmael, the hunted. But much more Ishmael the hunter. What's a Queequeg? What's a wife? The white whale must be hunted down. Queequeg must be just "KNOWN", then dropped into oblivion. . . .

AHAB SYMBOLIZES ATHEISM

You are some time before you are allowed to see the captain, Ahab: the mysterious Quaker. Oh, it is a God-fearing Quaker ship.

Ahab, the captain. The captain of the soul.

"I am the master of my fate,
I am the captain of my soul!"

Ahab! . . .

The gaunt Ahab, Quaker, mysterious person, only shows himself after some days at sea. There's a secret about him! What?

Oh, he's a portentous person. He stumps about on an ivory stump, made from sea-ivory. Moby Dick, the great white whale, tore off Ahab's leg at the knee, when Ahab was attacking him.

Quite right, too. Should have torn off both his legs, and a bit more besides.

But Ahab doesn't think so. Ahab is now a monomaniac. Moby Dick is his monomania. Moby Dick must DIE, or Ahab can't live any longer. Ahab is atheist by this.

All right.

THE *PEQUOD* SYMBOLIZES AMERICA'S DIVERSE POPULATION

This *Pequod*, ship of the American soul, has three mates.

1. Starbuck: Quaker, Nantucketer, a good responsible man of reason, forethought, intrepidity, what is called a dependable man. At the bottom, *afraid.*

2. Stubb: "Fearless as fire, and as mechanical." Insists on being reckless and jolly on every occasion. Must be afraid too, really.

3. Flask: Stubborn, obstinate, without imagination. To him "the wondrous whale was but a species of magnified mouse or water-rat——"

There you have them: a maniac captain and his three mates, three splendid seamen, admirable whalemen, first-class men at their job.

America! . . .

A maniac captain of the soul, and three eminently practical mates.

America!

Then such a crew. Renegades, castaways, cannibals: Ishmael, Quakers.

America!

Three giant harpooners, to spear the great white whale.

1. Queequeg, the South Sea Islander, all tattooed, big and powerful.

2. Tashtego, the Red Indian of the sea-coast, where the Indian meets the sea.

3. Daggoo, the huge black negro.

There you have them, three savage races, under the American flag, the maniac captain, with their great keen harpoons, ready to spear the white whale.

And only after many days at sea does Ahab's own boat-crew appear on deck. Strange, silent, secret, black-garbed Malays, fire-worshipping Parsees. These are to man Ahab's boat, when it leaps in pursuit of that whale.

What do you think of the ship *Pequod,* the ship of the soul of an American?

Many races, many peoples, many nations, under the Stars and Stripes. Beaten with many stripes.

Seeing stars sometimes.

And in a mad ship, under a mad captain, in a mad, fanatic's hunt.

For what?

For Moby Dick, the great white whale.

But splendidly handled. Three splendid mates. The whole thing practical, eminently practical in its working. American industry!

And all this practicality in the service of a mad, mad chase.

Melville manages to keep it a real whaling ship, on a real cruise, in spite of all fantastics. A wonderful, wonderful voyage. And a beauty that is so surpassing only because of the author's awful flounderings in mystical waters. He wanted to get metaphysically deep. And he got deeper than metaphysics. It is a surpassingly beautiful book, with an awful meaning, and bad jolts. . . .

THE SINKING OF THE *PEQUOD* SYMBOLIZES THE DOOM OF WHITE AMERICA

The fight with the whale is too wonderful, and too awful, to be quoted apart from the book. It lasted three days. The fearful sight, on the third day, of the torn body of the Parsee harpooner, lost on the previous day, now seen lashed on to the flanks of the white whale by the tangle of harpoon lines, has a mystic dream-horror. The awful and infuriated whale turns upon the ship, symbol of this civilized world of ours. He smites her with a fearful shock. And a few minutes later, from the last of the fighting whale-boats comes the cry: "'The ship! Great God, where is the ship?' Soon they, through dim, bewildering mediums, saw her sidelong fading phantom, as in the gaseous Fata Morgana; only the uppermost masts out of the water; while fixed by infatuation, or fidelity, or fate, to their once lofty perches, the pagan harpooners still maintained their sinking lookouts on the sea. And now concentric circles seized the lone boat itself, and all its crew, and each floating oar, and every lance-pole, and spinning, animate and inanimate, all round and round in one vortex, carried the smallest chip of the *Pequod* out of sight——"

The bird of heaven, the eagle, [first-century A.D. apostle to Jesus] St. John's bird, the Red Indian bird, the American, goes down with the ship, nailed by Tashtego's hammer, the hammer of the American Indian. The eagle of the spirit. Sunk!

"Now small fowls flew screaming over the yet yawning gulf; a sullen white surf beat against its steep sides; then all collapsed; and the great shroud of the sea rolled on as it rolled five thousand years ago."

So ends one of the strangest and most wonderful books in the world, closing up its mystery and its tortured symbolism. It is an epic of the sea such as no man has equalled; and it is a book of esoteric symbolism of profound significance, and of considerable tiresomeness.

But it is a great book, a very great book, the greatest book of the sea ever written. It moves awe in the soul.

The terrible fatality.

Fatality.

Doom.

Doom! Doom! Doom! Something seems to whisper it in the very dark trees of America. Doom!

Doom of what?

Doom of our white day. We are doomed, doomed. And the doom is in America. The doom of our white day.

Ah, well, if my day is doomed, and I am doomed with my day, it is something greater than I which dooms me, so I accept my doom as a sign of the greatness which is more than I am.

Melville knew. He knew his race was doomed. His white soul, doomed. His great white epoch, doomed. Himself, doomed. The idealist, doomed. The spirit, doomed.

The reversion. "Not so much bound to any haven ahead, as rushing from all havens astern."

That great horror of ours! It is our civilization rushing from all havens astern.

The last ghastly hunt. The White Whale.

What then is Moby Dick? He is the deepest blood-being of the white race; he is our deepest blood-nature.

And he is hunted, hunted, hunted by the maniacal fanaticism of our white mental consciousness. We want to hunt him down. To subject him to our will. And in this maniacal conscious hunt of ourselves we get dark races and pale to help us, red, yellow, and black, east and west, Quaker and fire-worshipper, we get them all to help us in this ghastly maniacal hunt which is our doom and our suicide.

The last phallic being of the white man. Hunted into the death of upper consciousness and the ideal will. Our blood-self subjected to our will. Our blood-consciousness sapped by a parasitic mental or ideal consciousness.

Hot-blooded sea-born Moby Dick. Hunted by monomaniacs of the idea. . . .

The *Pequod* went down. And the *Pequod* was the ship of the white American soul. She sank, taking with her negro and Indian and Polynesian, Asiatic and Quaker and good, businesslike Yankees and Ishmael: she sank all the lot of them.

Boom! as [American poet] Vachel Lindsay [1879–1931] would say.

To use the words of Jesus, IT IS FINISHED.

Consummatum est!

But *Moby Dick* was first published in 1851. If the Great White Whale sank the ship of the Great White Soul in 1851, what's been happening ever since?

Post-mortem effects, presumably.

Because, in the first centuries, Jesus was Cetus, the Whale. And the Christians were the little fishes. Jesus, the Redeemer, was Cetus, Leviathan. And all the Christians all his little fishes.

Moby-Dick Analyzes Nineteenth-Century Race Prejudice

Carolyn L. Karcher

Melville deliberately created the crew of the *Pequod* to reflect a racial mixture as diverse as the population of the United States, thereby allowing him to examine racial prejudice in American society. In this selection, Carolyn L. Karcher argues that each of the non-Caucasian characters reflects how Melville's contemporary Americans viewed people of color. Karcher details how Ishmael's confrontations with each of these characters force him to reevaluate his own attitudes and biases. Karcher is a professor at Temple University and the author of *The First Woman in the Republic: A Cultural Biography of Lydia Maria Child* and *Appeal in Favor of That Class of Americans Called Africans.*

In *Moby-Dick*, Melville envisages several possible dénouements to the American crisis over slavery, along with various answers to the question of whether individuals (and nations) help to weave their own destiny into the warp of necessity or are entirely caught in the threads of Fate's loom. "The Town-Ho's Story" offers Steelkilt's rebellion and its successful issue as one such dénouement. The main narrative of *Moby-Dick* offers another alternative to Ahab's destructive polity and the retribution it brings on the *Pequod*; for Ishmael, buoyed up by the coffin his friend Queequeg had ordered for himself and subsequently turned into a life buoy for the *Pequod*, miraculously escapes the cataclysm that overtakes his shipmates. As the means of Ishmael's escape betokens, his freely chosen friendship with Queequeg plays a conspicuous part in modifying his destiny, even though "those stage managers, the Fates," may have had the

Carolyn L. Karcher, *Shadow over the Promised Land: Slavery, Race, and Violence in Melville's America.* Baton Rouge: Louisiana State University Press, 1980. Copyright © 1980 by Louisiana State University Press. Reproduced by permission.

first and last word in sending him on this ill-starred voyage and ordaining its ending. Ishmael's friendship with Queequeg dramatizes the conclusions about racial prejudice that Melville had reached in *Redburn* and suggests that by embracing the Negro as an equal partner, American citizens might still avert the tempest that threatened to engulf their ship of state.

QUEEQUEG IS A SYMBOL OF AFRICAN AMERICANS

But before we can be sure of these racial implications, we must first determine whether Melville meant to identify Queequeg with the Negro—a question that has elicited lively debate among critics interested in Melville's racial attitudes. Those who credit Melville with enlightened racial views cite the cannibal as a fully developed and complimentary negroid characterization and emphasize the unprecedented egalitarianism of picturing a white man sharing a bed with a dark-skinned savage. Conversely, those who accuse Melville of racism point out that Queequeg is not an American Negro and theorize that Melville's deeply felt Marquesan [Marquesas Islands in southern Pacific Ocean near Tahiti] experience might have led to a "deification of Polynesians" without affecting his prejudices toward Africans or, for that matter, American Indians. What both sides seem to have missed—despite recognition of the way Queequeg telescopes Polynesian, American Indian, African, Islamic, and even Christian features and customs—is how deliberately Melville has blurred racial lines in portraying the savage, and how explicitly he has related Queequeg's ambiguously perceived racial identity to the issue of anti-Negro prejudice.

The most obvious sign that Melville intended to endow Queequeg with African attributes is the series of allusions that initially provoked the controversy. As critics of both schools have noted, Queequeg, though a native of the South Sea islands, incongruously worships a "little deformed image . . . exactly the color of a three days' old Congo baby," prompting Ishmael to call it his "negro idol." Furthermore, Queequeg and Ishmael later attract from passersby some of the hostile notice that Redburn imagines his ship's black steward would have received had he walked arm in arm with a white woman in the streets of New York. Since Ishmael and Queequeg are of the same sex, they are not mobbed, but they are greeted with stares and jeers. Ishmael pointedly comments that these taunts are due not to the outlandish figure Queequeg cuts—the citizens of New Bedford being "used to seeing cannibals like him in their streets"—but to the sight of two racially diverse "fellow beings" on such "companionable" terms. Underscoring the parallel with black-white relations in America, he drops the word "cannibal" to moralize outright: "as though a white man were anything more dignified than a whitewashed negro."

Hence it should be clear that Queequeg represents yet another of the composite racial figures that Melville created to undermine racial categories and to inculcate the lessons in racial tolerance and cultural relativism that he himself had learned in Typee. Through Ishmael's encounter with Queequeg, Melville shows how an educated young man of respectable social background learns to overcome his provincial bigotry and racial prejudices, just as he had earlier shown Redburn learning to overcome his anti-Negro feelings. With Ishmael, however, Melville takes the reader further than with Redburn, since he also calls into question for the first time the reality of the racial differences to which prejudice was generally ascribed in his day.

ISHMAEL CONFRONTS HIS OWN PREJUDICE

Even before Ishmael actually meets Queequeg, he confronts the problem of whether he "might be cherishing unwarrantable prejudices against this unknown harpooneer," with whom the landlord has proposed that he share the only remaining bed in the inn. The joke is that the well-defined prejudices Ishmael holds do not prevent the racial identity of his bedfellow from eluding him for the better part of a long chapter. Thus when Ishmael learns that the mysterious harpooneer "is actually engaged this blessed Saturday night, or rather Sunday morning, in peddling his head around this town," he does not connect this "cannibal business" with the previous revelation that the harpooneer is "a dark complexioned chap" who "eats nothing but steaks, and likes 'em rare." Instead, Ishmael expostulates with the landlord, unconsciously basing his claim to sagacity on color: "you'd better stop spinning that yarn to me—I'm not green." Accentuating the racial implications of this pun, the landlord's answering pun—"May be not . . . but I rayther guess you'll be done *brown* if that ere harpooneer hears you a slanderin' his head"—hints at the first lessons Ishmael will learn on being thrown together with Queequeg: that color prejudice is a two-way street and color itself a treacherous criterion on which to predicate anyone's identity, let alone his worth.

Ishmael's continued obtuseness regarding Queequeg's racial identity becomes more significant when the very sight of the cannibal fails to enlighten him. At the first view of Queequeg's "dark, purplish, yellow" face, "here and there stuck over with large, blackish looking squares," Ishmael supposes that "he's been in a fight, got dreadfully cut, and here he is, just from the surgeon." On perceiving that the black squares on Queequeg's cheeks are not "sticking-plasters," but "stains of some sort or other," Ishmael takes Queequeg for a "white man . . . who, falling among the cannibals, had been tattooed by them." He moralizes: "And what is it, thought I, after all! It's only his outside; a man can be honest in any sort of skin." Ironically, Ishmael has not meant to articulate a protest against color-consciousness.

Still under the misapprehension that Queequeg is a "white man," Ishmael struggles to explain how a white could have acquired such an "unearthly complexion." Echoing the scientific debates about whether racial features resulted from the influence of climate or from primordial biological differences, he wavers between two theories—that "the sun . . . produced these extraordinary effects upon the skin," or alternatively, that the stranger's distinctive skin color might arise from some deeper cause than climate: "I never heard of a hot sun's tanning a white man into a purplish yellow one." The "bald purplish head" that the stranger reveals on taking off his beaver hat frightens Ishmael more than his discolored tattooed skin, perhaps because it looks "for all the world like a mildewed skull"—just such a mildewed skull, in fact, as American archaeologists and ethnologists were currently disinterring from Indian burial grounds as a means of determining the racial character of America's aboriginal population. Hitherto curious enough to master his alarm, Ishmael now feels ready to bolt from the room. He accounts for his terror by remarking, "Ignorance is the parent of fear, and being completely nonplussed and confounded about the stranger, I confess I was now as much afraid of him as if it was the devil himself."

Once again, however, this broad-minded interpretation of racial prejudice ironically precedes Ishmael's realization that Queequeg is not a white man gone native, but an "abominable savage" from the South Seas—a fact that only becomes "quite plain" to him after Queequeg has completely undressed, disclosing a body tattooed from head to foot. Not until Queequeg has sprung upon him crying "Who-e debel you?," bringing the landlord to the rescue, does Ishmael belatedly digest the intuitions he has had about how irrelevant a man's skin color is to his character, and why people of different skin color fear each other as devils: "What's all this fuss I have been making about, thought I to myself—the man's a human being just as I am: he has just as much reason to fear me, as I have to be afraid of him."

ISHMAEL CHANGES HIS PERCEPTION ABOUT RACE

Overcoming color prejudice is but the initial stage of the transformation Ishmael undergoes. Once he removes his racial coloring glasses, Ishmael begins to see his savage bedfellow in another light, which in turn affects his perceptions of his white countrymen. The first breakthrough occurs when Ishmael realizes that the cannibal is in fact behaving "in not only a civil but a really kind and charitable way" toward him. By the next morning, Ishmael has also become aware of the unflattering contrast between his own "great rudeness" in staring at Queequeg and "watching all his toilette motions" as if he were an animal in the zoo, and Queequeg's "civility and consideration" in offering to leave the room so that Ishmael can dress in privacy. This leads Ishmael to question the appropriateness of the terms "savage" and "civilized" and to conclude that savages may be more "civilized" in certain respects than so-called "civilized" peoples: "Thinks I, Queequeg . . . this is a very civilized overture; but, the truth is, these savages have an innate sense of delicacy, say what you will; it is marvellous how essentially polite they are." Although Ishmael proceeds to regale the reader with a description of how Queequeg commences "dressing at top by donning his beaver hat" and then, "minus his trowsers," crushes himself "boots in hand, and hat on— under the bed . . . to be private when putting on his boots," his sense of Queequeg's idiosyncracies soon gives way to a growing appreciation of the savage's human qualities.

On joining the other sailors at breakfast, Ishmael already views the difference between them and Queequeg as one of degree, rather than kind. Whereas earlier he had tried to classify Queequeg as "white" or "savage," he now foregoes these racial categories altogether and distinguishes among the sailors only on the basis of their sun tans:

> This young fellow's healthy cheek is like a sun-toasted pear in hue, and would seem to smell almost as musky; he cannot have been three days landed from his Indian voyage. That man next him looks a few shades lighter; you might say a touch of satin wood is in him. In the complexion of a third still lingers a tropic tawn, but slightly bleached withal; *he* doubtless has tarried whole weeks ashore. But who could show a cheek like Queequeg? which, barred with various tints, seemed like the Andes' western slope, to show forth in one array, contrasting climates, zone by zone.

Queequeg's uniqueness, in other words, consists not in being "colored," as opposed to white (or purplish yellow, as opposed to another shade), but in being a compendium of the colors produced by various climates (apparently Ishmael has opted for the climatic explanation of racial differences).

Similarly, when Ishmael goes on to compare Queequeg's bearing and manners with those of his compeers, he no longer dwells on "Queequeg's peculiarities here; how he eschewed coffee and hot rolls, and applied his undivided attention to beefsteaks, done rare," serving himself with his harpoon. Instead, what impresses Ishmael is how much more poised Queequeg looks than the American sailors. They, in their native land, sit "at a social breakfast table—all of the same calling, all of kindred tastes—looking round as sheepishly at each other as though they had never been out of sight of some sheepfold among the Green Mountains." Queequeg, twenty thousand miles away from home and amid people whose language he can barely speak, presides "at the head of the table . . . as cool as an icicle."

In the next chapter, where Ishmael confronts the cross section of nations and races thronging the streets of New Bedford, his astonishment "at first catching a glimpse of so outlandish an individual as Queequeg circulating among the polite society of a civilized town" entirely evaporates. He remarks:

> In thoroughfares nigh the docks, any considerable seaport will frequently offer to view the queerest looking nondescripts from foreign parts. Even in Broadway and Chestnut streets, Mediterranean mariners will sometimes jostle the affrighted ladies. Regent street is not unknown to Lascars and Malays; and at Bombay, in the Apollo Green, live Yankees have often scared the natives. . . . In New Bedford, actual cannibals stand chatting at street corners; savages outright;

many of whom yet carry on their bones unholy flesh. It makes a stranger stare.

Lumping Mediterranean mariners and Yankees with Lascars and Malays, Ishmael jolts us into realizing, as *he* now does, that we are as anomalous to foreign peoples as they are to us—indeed perhaps more so, since the Lascars and Malays in London seem to attract no notice from the British, and the savages in jaded New Bedford go unheeded except by strangers, whereas in Bombay "live Yankees have often scared the natives." He also implies that no set of racial traits is inherently stranger than any other; that the strangeness, in short, is in the eye of the beholder. Thus a white seaman from Spain or Italy can seem more fearsome to an American lady who has never seen one than a cannibal does to a native of New Bedford. Ishmael delivers the final blow to his countrymen's ethnocentrism and color consciousness by asserting that what the reader will find "still more curious, certainly more comical" than all the dark-skinned "Feegeeans, Tongatabooans, Erromanggoans, Pannangians, and Brighggians" he will run across in New Bedford, is the spectacle of the "green Vermonters and New Hampshire men" who descend on the town by the score "all athirst for gain and glory" in the untried career of whaling: "Many are as green as the Green Mountains whence they come. . . . Look there! that chap strutting round the corner. He wears a beaver hat and swallow-tailed coat, girdled with a sailor-belt and sheath-knife. Here comes another with a sou'wester and a bombazine cloak." The analogy with Queequeg in his beaver hat is unmistakable, as is the moral, driven home in the following paragraph, that the South Sea savage who dons his boots under the bed is intrinsically no more ludicrous than the homegrown "bumpkin dandy" who mows his native acres "in buckskin gloves" during the dog days, "for fear of tanning his hands."

The change in Ishmael's perceptions, resulting in this sophisticated cultural relativism, culminates when he is able to discern the nobility of character underlying Queequeg's bizarre exterior:

> Savage though he was, and hideously marred about the face—at least to my taste—his countenance yet had a something in it which was by no means disagreeable. You cannot hide the soul. Through all his unearthly tattooings, I thought I saw the traces of a simple honest heart; and in his large, deep eyes,

fiery black and bold, there seemed tokens of a spirit that would dare a thousand devils. And besides all this, there was a certain lofty bearing about the Pagan, which even his uncouthness could not altogether maim. He looked like a man who had never cringed and never had had a creditor.

Not only does Ishmael overlook the disfigurements that had previously repelled him; he has also come to realize that his own distaste for tattooing is as ethnocentric as Queequeg's preference for it. But Ishmael's most radical departure from the racial prejudice that had originally distorted Queequeg into a devil in his eyes consists in ascribing phrenological [the study of the shape and size of the cranium as an indicator of character and mental faculties] excellence to Queequeg's negroid cranial conformation, with its retreating forehead and projecting brow, and identifying it with George Washington's: "certain it was his head was phrenologically an excellent one. It may seem ridiculous, but it reminded me of General Washington's head, as seen in the popular busts of him. It had the same long regularly graded retreating slope from above the brows, which were likewise very projecting, like two long promontories thickly wooded on top. Queequeg was George Washington cannibalistically developed." We need only recall that nineteenth-century Americans placed Washington side by side with Shakespeare at the pinnacle of human evolution—and consigned the African cannibal to its nadir—to measure the distance Ishmael has traveled.

THE SIGNIFICANCE OF ISHMAEL'S FRIENDSHIP WITH QUEEQUEG

Paralleling Ishmael's intellectual growth is the maturation of his acquaintance with Queequeg into a friendship destined to alter the course of his life. When Ishmael accepts Queequeg as his bedfellow with the famous words, "Better sleep with a sober cannibal than a drunken Christian," he carries the principles of racial tolerance and egalitarianism to what Redburn had recognized as their logical conclusion—vindicating "amalgamation." Ishmael, however, goes a step beyond Redburn; for he actually practices what he preaches and contracts a "marriage" with someone of another race symbolically associated with America's twin pariahs, the Negro and the Indian.

The insistent matrimonial imagery describing Ishmael's budding friendship with his new bedfellow has drawn much comment, both for its homosexual and its racial overtones. Whatever sexual predilections it may indicate in Melville, he knew he could get away with dramatizing a happy interracial marriage by disguising it as a male comradeship which his public would not dare interpret as homosexual. The crucial fact about Melville's imagery, after all, is that it elevates the taboo relationship between a white and a nonwhite to the plane of a legal marriage between equals—and a love marriage at that. Except when Ishmael, under the influence of his "unwarrantable prejudices," worries about having a strange harpooneer "tumble in upon me at midnight" with no way of knowing "from what vile hole he had been coming," Melville's jokes about the relationship are never merely bawdy. On the contrary, Ishmael and Queequeg consummate their friendship in the landlord's own conjugal bed, where their union issues in a "hatchet-faced baby" (Queequeg's tomahawk-calumet); Queequeg holds Ishmael in a "bridegroom clasp . . . as though naught but death should part us twain" (which indeed proves to be the case); Queequeg pronounces himself "married" to Ishmael, according to "his country's phrase"; Queequeg and Ishmael lie abed chatting in their "hearts' honeymoon" like "some old couples"; and Ishmael at last sees "how elastic our stiff prejudices grow when love once comes to bend them."

Beyond its propagandistic function of vindicating interracial marriage, the narrative significance of Ishmael's friendship with Queequeg lies in symbolizing the commitment that Ishmael makes, through Queequeg, to loving his fellow man and acknowledging the tie that binds him to the rest of humanity. This commitment, which will later protect Ishmael against succumbing entirely to Ahab's hate-driven pursuit of the white whale, initially rescues him from the mood of misanthropic despair that had impelled him to go to sea as an antidote to "methodically knocking people's hats off" and a "substitute for pistol and ball."

Moby-Dick and the Spirit of Revolution

Mark Niemeyer

Mark Niemeyer explains that Melville uses *Moby-Dick* to explore the ideals of American democracy while portraying Captain Ahab as a misguided revolutionary. Niemeyer shows how the many ethnic backgrounds of the crew of the *Pequod* represent American democracy, with each member overcoming cultural prejudices to work together. However, what they are working toward, the hunt for Moby Dick, is revealed to be a selfish, prideful quest, which goes against the ideals of democracy. Niemeyer has written extensively on nineteenth-century American literature.

Both the democratic and the revolutionary ideals which filled Melville at the time of the composition of *Moby-Dick* can be seen represented throughout the novel which [literary critic] Milton R. Stern characterizes as "an act of art against totalitarianism." Among the novel's characters, it is Ishmael and Ahab who most consistently embody and support these concepts. Ishmael offers an optimistic vision of the democratic ideal; Ahab embodies the extreme form of revolutionary zeal. In the very first chapter of the book, in fact, the reader learns that though he is not a novice sailor, Ishmael has no desire to have any position of power on the ships whose crews he joins. His philosophizing on the subject suggests a profoundly democratic view of the situation of man in the world: "What of it, if some old hunks of a sea-captain orders me to get a broom and sweep down the decks? . . . Who aint a slave? Tell me that." First of all, Ishmael has no desire for power over others, and second, he does not believe that those in positions of power are in genuinely superior stations. He even fancies, using his game-

Mark Niemeyer, "*Moby-Dick* and the Spirit of Revolution," *The Critical Response to Herman Melville's* Moby-Dick, edited by Kevin J. Hayes. Westport, CT: Greenwood Press, 1994. Copyright © 1994 by Kevin J. Hayes. Reproduced by permission.

some logic, that on board a ship the common sailors (spend-ing most of their time before the mast) have a better situa-tion than that of the officers: "for the most part the Com-modore on the quarter-deck gets his atmosphere at second hand from the sailors on the forecastle. He thinks he breathes it first; but not so." The thought leads to more gen-eral interpretations, this time with political undertones: "In much the same way do the commonalty lead their leaders in many other things, at the same time that the leaders little suspect it." Ishmael believes that it is the masses who often do, in fact, direct the affairs of society.

QUEEQUEG AND THE CREW REPRESENT DEMOCRACY

The narrator's comments on Queequeg reveal that Ishmael sees the cannibal as a natural democrat. In chapter ten, Ish-mael notes that Queequeg's profile reminds him of "General Washington's head, as seen in the popular busts of him," thus of America's greatest Revolutionary War hero. And Queequeg's own history is that of an abdication of monar-chical powers. The son of an island king, Queequeg is en-titled one day to inherit the crown of his father, but having run away, as Ishmael notes, "They had made a harpooneer of him, and that barbed iron was in lieu of a sceptre now." Later, Queequeg proves his broad democratic concern for others by saving a man (who had just previously mocked him) when he is swept overboard. Ishmael offers a generous interpretation of the harpooner's view of his own act in as-serting that Queequeg "seemed to be saying to himself—'It's a mutual, joint-stock world, in all meridians. We cannibals must help these Christians'." Whether these thought[s] really passed through Queequeg's mind is irrelevant. Ishmael is desirous of seeing the world as a functioning and caring democracy. . . .

THE VARIOUS SHIPS REVEAL DIFFERENT STATES OF POLITICAL UNREST

Ishmael's view of the great democratic spirit among whale-men, however, is somewhat rose-colored. If in any context democracy is not the model of organization, it is at sea. As Ishmael himself realizes, the captain of a ship is "the ab-solute dictator." The only time sailors approach a genuinely democratic situation which relieves them from the dictator-ial power of their captain's command is either when they somehow wrest control from his hands or when the captain's attention is diverted in such a fashion as to afford them a sort of de facto freedom. In fact, *Moby-Dick* presents the reader with a seething world, and the theme of the usurpation of power (and thus revolution) is ubiquitous [present everywhere or in several places simultaneously]. A look at the situation aboard some of the ships that the *Pequod* encounters during its voyage can help demonstrate this point. None of the nine whalers that Ahab and his crew meet can be said to display fully the traditional order, discipline and competence in which the captain is in undisputed command of his vessel, his crew, and his mission. For example, though Ishmael knows little of the *Goney*, the first ship they meet, the craft's "spectral appearance," its spars and rigging "like the thick branches of trees furred over with hoar-frost," its "long-bearded look-outs," and "strange captain" suggest an irregular state of affairs similar to the slovenly, haunted demeanor of the *San Domonick* in Melville's later work, "Benito Cereno." Whatever the cause for the vessel's state, things are not shipshape aboard the *Goney*.

Other whalers met by the *Pequod*, however, present clearer evidence of a loss of control by their respective captains. As Ishmael reveals in Chapter 54, a mutiny had, in fact, taken place on board the *Town-Ho*, the next ship encountered by the *Pequod*. The insurrection, sparked by the abusive exercise of authority on the part of the mate, is described in terms suggesting an implicit comparison with the French revolutionaries of 1848. The mutinous crew members "succeeded in gaining the forecastle deck, where, hastily slewing about three or four large casks in a line with the windlass, these sea-Parisians entrenched themselves behind the barricade." While the mutineers are finally subdued and agree to cooperate to a certain degree with the captain, unlike their French counterparts, they eventually escape the severest punishment, as Steelkilt, the organizer of the rebellion, seems to hold some unexplainable power over the captain of the *Town-Ho*. When the ship reaches port after their act of defiance, Steelkilt and "all but five or six of the foremast-men deliberately deserted among the palms; eventually, as it turned out, seizing a large double war-canoe of the savages, and setting sail for some other harbor."

The third ship that the *Pequod* meets is the *Jeroboam*. While Captain Mayhew is ostensibly in charge of his craft, the narrator relates that a religious fanatic known as Gabriel, who has refused to perform his normal duties, has gained such a sway over the other crew members that they support his insubordination to the point of defying the captain: "So strongly did he work upon his disciples among the crew, that at last in a body they went to the captain and told him if Gabriel was sent from the ship, not a man of them would remain." Captain Mayhew bows to this pressure from his crew, apparently true believers in Gabriel's religious vision of events (perhaps suggesting political idealism), thus permitting a mutiny in all but name to be tolerated on board his vessel.

The power of the captain of the *Bouton de Rose* is also usurped partially when Stubb and the English-speaking chief mate of the French vessel concoct "a little plan for both circumventing and satirizing the Captain, without his at all dreaming of distrusting their sincerity." With this plan, the Guernsey man (and the rest of the crew of the *Bouton de Rose*, for that matter) are freed from executing the captain's unpleasant order to process the rotting and stinking carcasses tied to the ship's sides, and Stubb is able surreptitiously to recover some of the valuable ambergris from the whale that he agrees, as a supposed favor, to tow away for the thankful (and duped) captain of the *Bouton de Rose*. The crew thus rids itself of an oppressive obligation, which was no less despotic having been given in ignorance by a captain who did not know that long-dead whales would yield little or no oil.

The spirit aboard the *Bachelor* is lighter and merrier than that on any other ship the *Pequod* meets. The *Bachelor* has met with such good fortune that every available space is crammed with barrels full of oil or spermaceti, and the Nantucket ship is preparing to head home. But even on this commercially successful vessel, suggesting competence and order, things get somewhat out of control. So caught up in the celebration of their fortune, the sailors (among other acts of revelry) break apart the try-works under the apparently approving eye of a captain who seems more a lord of misrule than a maintainer of discipline: "others of the ship's company were tumultuously busy at the masonry of the try-works, from which the huge pots had been removed. You would have almost thought they were pulling down the cursed Bastile, such wild cries they raised, as the now useless brick and mortar were being hurled into the sea." The allusion to the attack on the Bastille prison (once again referring to the French revolution of 1789) clearly suggests a revolutionary disruption of the normal power hierarchy on board the *Bachelor* rather than simply a mood of festivity. All of these examples present captains who, generally because of a certain popular uprising of sentiment among their crews, no longer exercise a complete control over their vessels or missions. And even though the other ships met by the *Pequod* do not display what can be considered as clear examples of mutiny, they do, to a greater or lesser extent, portray situations in which the captain's power and authority has been diminished or diverted, in which a degradation or temporary cessation of the normal operating procedures on board has taken place.

AHAB BECOMES A REVOLUTIONARY LEADER

A similar disruption takes place aboard the *Pequod*. Here, ironically, it is the captain, who forces the overturning of normal structures. Indeed, as the narrator states, Ahab, an archetypal revolutionary leader in its most extreme form, is aware of the radical nature of his action and its possible consequences: "he had indirectly laid himself open to the unanswerable charge of usurpation; and with perfect impunity, both moral and legal, his crew if so disposed, and to that end competent, could refuse all further obedience to him, and even violently wrest from him the command." Ahab's real usurpation in his design to hunt the white whale, however, since he has, in fact, obtained (or extracted) the assent and participation of the crew, a sort of "multiracial proliteriat," is against the owners of the *Pequod* who have financed the voyage. In one of the later disputes between the captain and Starbuck, who frequently defends common sense and conservatism, Ahab declares, "Owners, owners? Thou are always prating to me, Starbuck, about those miserly owners, as if the owners were my conscience. But look ye, the only real owner of anything is its commander; and hark ye, my conscience is in this ship's keel." Ahab's total disregard for the owners is, among more general feelings of defiance, a refusal to recognize property rights within the context of a capitalistic system, one of the central causes of the people's misery, of course, according to nineteenth-century revolutionaries.

In fact, in an early description of the crew, Ishmael compares them to "An Anacharsis Clootz deputation from all the isles of the sea, and all the ends of the earth, accompanying Old Ahab in the Pequod to lay the world's grievances before that bar from which not very many of them ever come back." The reference to Anacharsis Cloots links Ahab with the Prussian nobleman, who, having come to Paris in 1776, became a fervent supporter of the Revolution from its beginning and espoused its more radical positions. Cloots named himself "orator of the human race" and "citizen of humanity." In June 1790 he led a heterogenous group of foreigners (much like the crew aboard the *Pequod*) to the Constituent Assembly in order to demonstrate symbolically the world's support for the Revolution. Later Cloots personally financed the arming of a group of between forty and fifty fighters in the sacred cause against tyranny. (This private initiative can also be seen as paralleling Ahab's muster and rallying of his crew to aid him in the realization of his goal.) By the summer of 1792, the pride of this confirmed radical had reached new summits; one of the founders of the cult of reason, Cloots declared himself the personal enemy of Jesus Christ and rejected all revealed religions, thus displaying another similarity to Ahab in the captain's defiance of God. Unfortunately for the enthusiastic revolutionary, but significant as a final parallel to the fate of Ahab and his crew, Cloots was eventually arrested and subsequently guillotined on 24 March 1794 becoming a victim of the very fanaticism he had helped encourage.

AHAB'S CONFLICTING POLITICS LEAD TO HIS DESTRUCTION

A more personal, and perhaps more touching, suggestion of Ahab's democratic feelings is the relationship which begins to develop between the captain and Pip near the end of the novel and the emotions which this relationship evokes in the captain. While the madness of the two characters certainly provides strong grounds for affinity, more is suggested in Ahab's comments to Pip at the end of chapter 125: "Come, then, to my cabin. Lo! ye believers in gods all goodness, and in man all ill, lo you! see the omniscient gods oblivious of suffering man; and man, though idiotic, and knowing not what he does, yet full of the sweet things of love and gratitude. Come! I feel prouder leading thee by thy black hand, than though I grasped an Emperor's!" Not only does Ahab's taking of Pip's hand provide a concrete symbol of the captain's democratic feelings, but the relationship itself, and specifically Pip's concern for Ahab, seems to restore the captain's confidence in the fundamental goodness of humanity, the very basis of democratic and revolutionary philosophy. And even if one is not lead by such a scene to believe in a genuinely egalitarian aspect of Ahab's character (and there are serious, if not overwhelming, reasons to doubt such a conclusion), it suggests that the monomaniacal captain may at least enjoy the image of himself as a magnanimous democrat.

One contrast to the view of Ahab as democrat can be seen in the frequent references to the captain's royal aspect. As these comparisons are made by Ishmael, the same motivation, at least to a certain extent, can be attributed to them as to the narrator's other allusions to nobility: they are meant to suggest grandeur and honor. For example, when Ishmael contemplates Ahab sitting on the stool whose legs are made of narwhale tusks, as were, he claims, the thrones of Danish kings in former times, he asks, "How could one look at Ahab then, seated on that tripod of bones, without bethinking him of the royalty it symbolized?" In Ahab's case, though, the significance of these comparisons to royalty is not so simple. When Ishmael refers to Flask as entering "King Ahab's presence," he is obviously trying to communicate the captain's distance from even his officers, a haughtiness lost on none of the crew members. Indeed, the potential arrogance and sentiments of superiority of revolutionary leaders such as Cloots (who wisely dropped his title of Baron soon after beginning his revolutionary activities) is just one aspect of their characters which Melville saw as similar to the very rulers they hoped to depose.

The presentation of this second face of revolution, in fact, is an important implicit censure of radicalism which allows a possible interpretation of *Moby-Dick* as offering a politically conservative message. When Ahab sees himself as greater than the gods, for example, he reveals both his determination and his hubris. Starbuck sees the hypocritical aspect of Ahab's stance: "Who's over him, he cries;—aye, he would be a democrat to all above; look how he lords it over all below!" Ahab may have convinced himself of certain democratic motivations in his revolutionary actions, of the idea that somehow he was not pursuing Moby Dick for just his own personal ends, but, at the same time, he clearly sees himself as superior to the masses he leads. His later comparison between himself as a "Greek god" and the carpenter as a "blockhead" only states the case more crudely. In the captain of the *Pequod*, the reader is presented with a leader dedicated to an ideal, not to the amelioration [improvement] of his fellow man's situation. Ahab's upbraiding of one of the crew for "not steering inflexibly enough" is just another indication of commitment coupled with a corresponding lack of humanity. Indeed, the problem with Ahab's mission, and the extent to which it can be seen as an implicit criticism of the supposedly democratic goals of revolutionaries, is its fundamentally "private" and fanatical nature.

Ahab's conduct becomes so extreme, in fact, that, at Starbuck's suggestion, the crew does make an attempt at mutiny, a counterrevolution, in a sense, aimed at giving up the chase of Moby Dick and heading homeward. As the first mate briefly seizes the revolutionary current from Ahab, he acts out perhaps his finest moment; for once, Starbuck does not cower, but stands up for the ideals he believes in, for what he feels is in the best interest of the crew and the ship. Burning harpoon in hand, Ahab, however, thwarts this attempted reaction: "Petrified by his aspect, and still more shrinking from the fiery dart that he held, the men fell back in dismay." With resigned fatalism, Starbuck later reflects that Ahab "would fain kill all the crew." Despite the obvious danger, however, once Moby Dick has been sighted and the chase begun, the crew begins to rally to the leader they had doubted. While this renewed confidence is certainly due in part to the adrenaline flow triggered by the hunt, its effect is undeniable: "Whatever pale fears and forebodings some of them might have felt before; these were not only now kept out of sight through the growing awe of Ahab; but they were broken up, and on all sides routed, as timid prairie hares that scatter before the bounding bison." When the moment of truth arrives, the whalemen of the *Pequod*, whatever their mixed motivations, choose to fight at the side of their captain. As Milton R. Stern notes, "For Melville, the other side of the coin of democracy is that individuals in the organized mass cannot resist the charismatic leader of the great crusade."

The unfortunate result of the hunt, of course, is the death of Ahab and of all the members of the crew except Ishmael. The last image of the novel presents the arm of the American Indian Tashtego hammering a replacement red flag (or vane) to the masthead of the ship, already almost completely underwater. . . .

Viewing the work from a political point of view, the ending can, I believe, be . . . coherently interpreted [as follows]. First, Melville can be seen as simply mirroring the tragic end of the French revolutions (both of 1789 and 1848), as well as of the other revolutions of 1848, in their deadly toll and in their complete failure to achieve their more idealistic goals. Second, if he is criticizing these revolutionary activities, it is more with regret that their ideals never were fully realizable in this world and could, unfortunately, become distorted or perverted by their leaders. It is in this spirit of embracing the revolutionary challenge to accepted systems that Melville praised [nineteenth-century American novelist Nathaniel] Hawthorne for saying "NO! in thunder," and it is in this identity with the radical mind that Melville wrote to Hawthorne . . . of the probability of his developing the reputation for supporting "ruthless democracy." Finally, how else can one interpret Melville's later confession to his fellow writer, just three days after the American publication of *Moby-Dick*, "I have written a wicked book, and feel spotless as the lamb," than as an affirmation of Ahab's mad pursuit of a radical goal which middle-class readers would be sure to reject? Despite my own argument, I do not see *Moby-Dick* as a conscious evocation of (or support of) Marxist [the political and economic theories of nineteenth-century German philosopher Karl Marx, which predicted the overthrow of capitalism and the eventual forming of a classless society] (or even necessarily political) revolutionary ideals. I do, however, see it as an expression (highlighted, in fact, by a certain number of consciously radical allusions) of that tension between desire and necessity. . . which resulted in the presentation of what for Melville must have been the irresistibly seductive spirit of revolution.

Moby-Dick Reflects Melville's Political Stance

Alan Heimert

In this essay Alan Heimert claims that *Moby-Dick* presents Melville's analysis of American political policy. Published in 1851, a decade before the start of the Civil War, *Moby-Dick* explores the political tensions over both the slavery issue and concerns Americans had over the United States' continuing imperialism. War with Mexico ended with enormous gains in territory for the United States, resulting in even more political turmoil over whether slavery would be allowed in these new territories. Melville set out to show the dangerous folly of both slavery and imperialism through the symbolic hunt for Moby Dick. Professor Heimert taught American literature at Harvard University and is the author of *Religion and the American Mind.*

In the process of canonizing Herman Melville as a major American writer, critics have generally failed to touch on the specific political context of his works. Yet *Moby-Dick* was produced in the very months of one of America's profoundest political crises: the controversy surrounding the "Compromise of 1850" [a series of measures passed by the U.S. Congress to form a compromise between states advocating slavery and those wishing to abolish slavery, especially regarding new territories of California, Utah, and New Mexico]. Recently [literary critic] Charles H. Foster re-examined *Moby-Dick* in terms of one aspect of this crisis. To Foster, Melville's recorded responses to the Fugitive Slave Law [laws penalizing U.S. marshals who did not seize runaway slaves or those who assisted them] suggest that *Moby-Dick* unfolded, and may be read on one level, as "a fable of dem-

Alan Heimert, "*Moby-Dick* and American Political Symbolism," *American Quarterly*, vol. XV, Winter 1963, pp. 498–506. Copyright © 1963 by The Johns Hopkins University Press. Reproduced by permission.

ocratic protest." But horror over slavery was but one ingredient—albeit the most familiar to students of literature—in an excitement which, in 1850, comprehended the nation's entire political life.

The crisis of 1850 marked the dramatic culmination of a complex series of political developments that had arrested national attention for nearly a decade. Melville himself had been deeply involved in debate over many of the vexing questions of the 1840s. As an associate of literary-political "Young America," he had joined in controversy over expansion, "imperialist" [a policy of acquiring territories in order to expand a country's domain] war and the character and future of the Democratic Party. When Melville addressed himself to American politics in the "Vivenza" section of *Mardi,* he showed himself unwilling to consider any single issue—even that of slavery—apart from the many others that impinged on the national consciousness. His contemporaries were likewise reluctant to consider the controversy over slavery as an isolated matter. The Compromise of 1850 itself was an artful (some said artificial) effort to preserve intellectual, as well as political, unity in a time of nearly revolutionary change.

America's ultimate concerns in this crucial epoch were expressed in a seemingly inexhaustible literature of politics—speeches, orations, sermons and editorials, nearly all published and circulated in incredible numbers. This material embodied not only political ideas, but an elaborate ritual and symbolism, much of which Melville drew upon in penning the satire of *Mardi.* It was against such a broad and intricate backdrop of political thought, speech and action—the full pattern, and not isolated threads—that *Moby-Dick* was composed in the explosive months of 1850.

THE SHIP AS A SYMBOL OF AMERICA

When in the 1840s the citizen of the United States pictured his nation's development and situation, he imagined the Republic as a ship, its history as a voyage. Often, too, he compared his country to that paradigm of his great-grandfathers, the children of Israel. It was to the nautical-political image that [nineteenth-century Unitarian theologian and antislavery activist] Theodore Parker, among others, turned for a sense of continuity amid changing circumstances:

> they stood to the right hand or the left, they sailed with much canvas or little, and swift or slow, as the winds and waves

> compelled: nay, sometimes the national ship "heaves to," and lies with her "head to the wind," regardless of her destination; but when the storm is blown resumes her course.

Parker was able to show that Israel's "course was laid toward a certain point," but in 1848 he could not so easily identify the "political destination" of America. To many other Americans, during the gathering storm of the Mexican War, the image of Canaan was equally unclear; for most the sweet fields beyond the flood were the peaceful land from which the nation had recklessly embarked.

To critics of America's political course, the Ship of State seemed to have rushed from all havens astern in 1845. The issue of Texas annexation presented itself to Whigs [the political party active 1834–1854; sought compromise on the slavery issue] as a question of "whether our old ship of state shall be launched upon an unknown sea—shall sail upon an unknown voyage." Then the ship's "captain" ran the vessel "into the whirlpool of the Mexican War," and it was feared the Ship would go down "'Deeper than plummet ever sounded,' carrying with it the last best hopes of the oppressed of mankind." By 1848 thoughtful citizens wondered if the analogy of ship and government, which had seemed to hold since the founding of the Federal Union . . . , remained tenable. In the peroration of *White-Jacket* Melville asked whether the crew and passengers of a commonwealth should be left so completely at the captain's mercy. . . .

THE *PEQUOD*'S CREW REPRESENTS A DIVERSE AMERICAN POPULATION

In the *Pequod* Melville created a ship strikingly similar to the vessels which rode the oratorical seas of 1850. It sails under a red flag, and its crew—in all its "democratic dignity"—comprises a "deputation from all the isles of the earth." But the *Pequod* is clearly reminiscent of [nineteenth-century American poet Henry Wadsworth] Longfellow's *Union* [a ship from a poem of the same name, symbolizing unity of diverse Americans]; it is put together of "all contrasting things" from the three sections of the United States: "oak and maple, and pine wood; iron, and pitch, and hemp." And the *Pequod* is manned (as we are reminded at each crucial moment in its career) by *thirty* isolatoes—all, Melville remarks, "federated along one keel."

The *Pequod's* mates, moreover, are "every one of them Americans; a Nantucketer, a Vineyarder, a Cape man." But of the three only one seems truly a New Englander or even a Northerner in terms either of the sectional iconography of the day or of Melville's own. Starbuck, who hails from the "prudent isle" of Nantucket and is ever-loyal to the commercial code of that island's "calculating people," is recognizably a Yankee. But good-humored Stubb seems a representative of that "essentially Western" spirit which Melville would attribute to the "convivial" frontiersman, [eighteenth-century American Revolutionary War hero] Ethan Allen. Stubb's speech is not in the Cape Cod idiom; it is studded with references to "broad-footed farmers" and images and chickens and milldams. For Stubb, harpooning a whale is "July's immortal Fourth," on which he yearns for "old Orleans whiskey, or old Ohio, or unspeakable Monongahela"— not the rum associated with the genuine Yankee. The "Vineyarder," the "very pugnacious" Flask, seems likewise closely related to that "fiery and intractable race" which Melville discovered in the south of Vivenza. Flask, who speaks of his "Martha's Vinyard plantation," reacts to whales in terms of the southern *code duello* [rules of duelling]:

> He seemed to think that the great Leviathans had personally and hereditarily affronted him; and therefore it was a sort of point of honor with him, to destroy them whenever encountered.

The harpooneers, finally, who so "generously" supply "the muscles" for the "native American" mates, are representatives of the three races on which each of the American sections, it might be said, had built its prosperity in the early nineteenth century. Stubb's squire is an Indian; Starbuck's comes from the Pacific islands. And Flask, perched precariously on Daggoo's shoulders, seems, like the southern economy itself, sustained only by the strength of the "imperial negro."

BIBLICAL REFERENCES SYMBOLIZE POLITICAL POLICIES

Ships and sailors were by no means the only images visible on the composite political canvas of 1850. Not unsurprisingly, considering America's intellectual and literary heritage, the mural was also filled with Scriptural incidents and characters. Not merely clergymen, but Whig congressmen and disturbed northern Democrats as well, had turned to the Old Testament when wielding their anti-imperialist jeremiads. "It is recorded every where, along the pathway of the world, in letters of glowing fire," cried an Albany orator: "The handwriting is on the wall. 'Mene, mene, tekel, up-harsin!'[a biblical riddle translated as "it has been counted and counted, weighed and divided"; refers to the king's deeds having been judged and found deficient resulting in his kingdom becoming divided]—is bursting upon the sight wherever nations or individuals are cherishing selfish aggrandisement above the everlasting right."

Out of the Old Testament too came an archetypal figure useful when portraying the dangers of Manifest Destiny [belief held by many Americans in the 1840s that the United States was destined to expand across the continent, by force if necessary]. As one Congressman explained while criticizing [eleventh president of the United States (1845–1849); precipitated the Mexican War, James Knox] Polk's expansionism, proof that "the sin of covetousness, and the curses consequent upon its indulgence, apply to nations as well as to individuals," could be found in the fact that "Ahab, King of Samaria" had been "made to repent in sackcloth" for his "usurpation of another's rights." In 1845 [nineteenth-century American antislavery activist and publisher] David Lee Child published a celebrated tract entitled *The Taking of Naboth's Vineyard, or History of the Texas Conspiracy.* Each of Polk's successive calls to "prosperity and glory" was invariably criticized as a "coveting of Naboth's Vineyard." So common was the likening of American invasion of other nations' rights to Ahab's aggressions that by 1848 [nineteenth-century American poet] James Russell Lowell, attacking the Mexican War in the *Biglow Papers,* saw no need to amplify when he alluded in his notes to "neighbor Naboths." In the same year Theodore Parker gave as the Old Testament "Scripture Lesson" for his famous sermon on the Mexican War (in which he referred to the siege of Tabasco as such "wanton butchery" that "none but a Pequod Indian could excuse it") the chronicle of Ahab's career in I Kings 21: 1–19. When Parker invoked the prophecy of Elijah that Ahab's dogs would one day lick his blood, he knew, better than Child three years earlier, that the "accident" President, James Knox Polk, was no true Ahab. Even during the Texas crisis, the "master-spirit of annexation" was, for thoughtful minds, none other than [nineteenth-century American statesman] John C. Calhoun. After [nineteenth-century U.S. Senator] Thomas Hart Benton was heard to bellow that "Inexorable HISTORY, with her pen of iron and tablets of brass" would write that Calhoun alone was "the author of the present war between the United States and Mexico," there was no longer any question as to whom the many improvers of the Ahab legend had in mind.

MELVILLE WARNS AGAINST U.S. POLICY OF IMPERIALISM

Melville first addressed himself to the problem of American imperialism in *Mardi,* where he devoted the better part of two chapters to the issue of Manifest Destiny. He echoes the oratorical allusions to Naboth's domain by describing the Caribbean lands, for which the Vivenzans "longed and lusted," as "gardens." Ahab himself is brought to mind in the proclamation read after the "inflammatory" stump speeches. Here Melville, speaking through a figure clearly intended as the young Democratic leader [attorney general of New York and son of eighth president of the United States (1837–1841)] John Van Buren, cautions the militant expansionists: "cheer not on the yelping pack too furiously. Hunters have been torn by their hounds." In treating of the possibility of "crimson republics . . . speeding to their culminations," Melville chooses a parallel from ancient Rome to remind Americans of the perilous course of empire:

> In chronicles of old, you read, sovereign-kings! that an eagle from the clouds presaged royalty to the fugitive Taquinoo. . . .

> In nations, sovereign-kings! there is a transmigration of souls; in you, is a marvelous destiny. The eagle of Romaro revives in your own mountain bird, and once more is plumed for her flight. Her screams are answered by the vauntful cry of a hawk; his red comb yet reeking with slaughter. And one East, one West, those bold birds may fly, till they lock pinions in the mid-most beyond.

> But, soaring in the sky over the nations that shall gather their broods under their wings, that bloody hawk may hereafter be taken for an eagle.

Melville's imaginary scroll is torn to shreds by the impatient mob—just as, in fact, a multitude of northern Democrats fulfilled the premonitions of those who warned, in 1847, that "A democracy without humanity is a herd of wolves." Whatever Melville's final judgments on the "fiery" Barnburners portrayed in *Mardi,* he obviously continued to question the imperialist ambitions of American Democracy. For when he came in *Moby-Dick* to write of "all the revolving panoramas

of empire on earth," Melville gave Ahab as an omen not Tar-
quin's imperial eagle, revived in the symbol of American liberty, but the other bloody bird, the conquering hawk.

THE WHALE AS A SYMBOL OF MANIFEST DESTINY

The pro-expansionists whom Melville satirized found no
single image adequate to the whole of their imperial aspirations. But the Whig Journal, the *Knickerbocker,* suggested
that the perfect embodiment of Manifest Destiny was "the
Great American Sea-Serpent." Implying that Democratic
spokesmen had in fact employed the symbol, the *Knickerbocker* caused its spread-eagle orator to proclaim:

> The Rocky Mountains are not more peculiarly our national
> property than the Sea-Serpent. Niagara Falls are not; the Mis-
> sissippi river is not; Mammoth Cave is not.

The "sea-serpent," which some claimed to have "sighted" in
New England waters in 1812, had curiously enough timed its
"reappearance" in the 1840s to coincide with a resurgence of
Northern concern over expansionism. The "Serpent" was to
have been the subject of Melville's articles for *Yankee Doodle*
in 1848; but [nineteenth-century American writer Evert A.]
Duyckinck ordered instead a lampoon of [hero of the Mexican
War and twelfth president of the United States (1849–1850)]
Zachary Taylor's dispatches. But the beast continued as a
topic of conversation in Melville's New York literary circle,
perhaps because in 1849 Eugene Batchelder, a self-conceived
Boston wit, published his *Romance of the Sea-Serpent.* His
verses connected the chase of the "serpent" with the advance
of Americans into Mexico and the Californian golden empire.
But like Melville, for whom in *Moby-Dick* Texas was a "Fast-
Fish" and Mexico a "Loose-Fish" but the White Whale himself
something more, so too did Batchelder ascribe transcendent
stature to the Serpent. To Batchelder this emblem of American empire seemed the very Leviathan of the Old Testament.

For critics and partisans alike, "Manifest Destiny" con-
jured up only the grandest of images. As the *Knickerbocker's*
"orator" explained, the "shaggy buffalo" of the prairie, the
"slumbering alligator" of the Everglades, and the "grissly
bear" of the Rockies was each impressive in its way, but only
"the Great American Sea-Serpent raises his blazing crest
high above all, majestic, unapproachable, and sublime
[large and impressive in size, scope, or extent]!" Here precisely was the Whig indictment of the apostles of Manifest

Destiny: they were causing America to forsake its household gods in a senseless quest for the sublime. Democratic pilots were maneuvering the national Ship from the course it had long pursued in safety, "well laden with rich and valuable cargoes." The Democracy was encouraging an "itinerant desire" in American breasts, making a people discontent with "familiar objects of devotion," and luring them from "the domestic altar" into worship of "strange idols" not unlike "the Baalim" of an earlier age. The Democratic prospect of empire was grand and vast, but the Whigs cherished their less-troubled bookkeeper's vision of national prosperity.

In deriding imperial ambitions the Whig literati hoped to exorcise sublimity with the same device they had long used "to contain the violence of Jacksonian [referring to Andrew Jackson, seventh president of the United States (1829–1837)] America." But the more astute Whig politicians knew that the appeal of the sublime—like that of Andrew Jackson himself—could not be burlesqued into insignificance. [Nineteenth-century American statesman] John Bell, for one, observed that Mexico fired the American imagination because there "nature exhibits herself in her most sublime and terrific, as well as in her more lovely and enchanting aspects." And such natural sublimity, Bell wisely perceived, was but the shadow of the greater "attractions" of empire itself—with its appeal to the American "passion for the grand, the vast, and the marvellous." Such thoughtful observers of American character did not deride the sublime; rather they reminded an aggressive Democracy that the imperial sublime, like the natural, has two faces. What seems enticingly sublime when viewed from afar, [nineteenth-century American historian] Alexander Stephens warned, might prove sublimely aweful when finally confronted:

> The mountain in the distance, clothed in its "Azure hue," looks all smooth and even; but experience as well as poetry tells us, it is the distance that gives "enchantment to the view." Surveyed at its base, in the gloomy shade of its august frown, . . . its surface is far from appearing even and smooth. Already we see its rocks—the high impending cliffs—the deep ravines—the frightful chasms. . . .

Or, as any of a host of orators might have said, the very thing that allured the Ship of State out of its accustomed ways might in the end prove the instrument of its destruction.

Chronology

1819

Born on August 1, in New York City, the third of eight children, to merchant Allan Melvill and Maria Gansevoort Melvill, daughter of a hero of the American Revolution.

1825

Enters New York Male High School, which he attends for four years.

1830

Allan Melvill's business fails and family moves to Albany. Herman attends Albany Academy.

1832

Allan Melvill dies, leaving family in debt. Herman begins a series of jobs to help the family, including bank clerk and helper on his brother's farm.

1832–1834

Sometime between 1832 and 1834, Maria Melvill adds an "e" to her last name, perhaps to distance herself from her deceased husband's business failures.

1835–1838

Melville continues his education at various high schools, helping with his family's finances by teaching.

1838

With family moves to Lansingburgh, near Albany, where he attends Lansingburgh Academy to study surveying and engineering.

1839

May 4, "Fragments from a Writing Desk" is published in the *Democratic Press and Lansingburgh Advertiser*. Melville joins the crew of a merchant ship, *Saint Lawrence*, on which he travels to Liverpool, England, and back. Teaches school in Greenbush, New York.

1841–1844

Melville signs on as a sailor aboard the whaler *Acushnet*, heading for the South Seas. He jumps ship in the Marquesas Islands, where he lives among the natives for a month. He joins the crew of a Nantucket whaler and is discharged in Hawaiian Islands. Enlists in the U.S. Navy in Honolulu and sails as a seaman on the frigate *United States*. Returns to Boston on October 4, 1844, is discharged and rejoins his family in Lansingburgh.

1846

Publishes his first novel, *Typee*, about his adventures in the South Seas.

1847

Publishes *Omoo*. Marries Elizabeth Shaw, daughter of Lemuel Shaw, chief justice of the Massachusetts Supreme Court.

1847–1850

Publishes several articles and reviews.

1849

Publishes *Mardi* and *Redburn*. Son Malcolm is born.

1850

Publishes *White-Jacket*. Moves family to Arrowhead, a farm in Massachusetts, where he begins friendship with novelist Nathaniel Hawthorne, who lives nearby.

1851

Publishes *Moby-Dick*. Son Stanwix is born.

1852

Publishes *Pierre*.

1853

Daughter Elizabeth is born.

1853–1856

Publishes fourteen stories and sketches in several prestigious literary magazines.

1855

Publishes *Israel Potter* in book form, after it has been serialized in *Putnam's Monthly Magazine*. Daughter Francis is born.

1856

Publishes *The Piazza Tales,* a collection of five pieces from Putnam's, including "Bartleby, The Scrivner" (1853). Failing health prompts Melville to take a trip to Europe and the Near East.

1857

Publishes *The Confidence-Man.* Returns to the United States.

1857–1860

In order to support his family, Melville undertakes three lecture tours: "Statues in Rome" (1857–1858), "The South Seas" (1858–1859), and "Traveling" (1859–1860). In 1860, he fails in his attempts to publish a volume of poetry.

1863

Sells Arrowhead and moves his family to New York City.

1866

Publishes a poetry collection, *Battle-Pieces and Aspects of the War.* Melville becomes the District Inspector of the United States Customs Service at the port of New York.

1867

Melville's wife, Elizabeth, discusses with her minister her unhappy marriage and desire to leave her husband. Melville's son Malcolm dies.

1876

Melville's uncle pays for the publication of *Clarel.*

1885

Melville resigns his position with Customs.

1886

Son Stanwix dies.

1888

Privately publishes *John Marr and Other Stories* in an edition of twenty-five copies.

1891

Privately publishes *Timoleon* in an edition of twenty-five copies. On September 28, Melville dies. He leaves behind the manuscript for *Billy Budd,* which is published for the first time in 1924.

FOR FURTHER RESEARCH

ABOUT MELVILLE

Warner Berthoff, *The Example of Melville*. Princeton, NJ: Princeton University Press, 1962.

Edgar A. Dryden, *Melville's Thematics of Form: The Great Art of Telling the Truth*. Baltimore: Johns Hopkins University Press, 1968.

John Fentress Gardner, *Melville's Vision of America: A New Interpretation of* Moby Dick. New York: Myrin Institute, 1977.

Elizabeth Hardwick, *Herman Melville*. New York: Viking, 2000.

A.R. Humphreys, *Herman Melville*. New York: Grove Press, 1962.

Robert Lee, *Herman Melville: Reassessments*. Totowa, NJ: Barnes & Noble, 1984.

Robert S. Levine, ed., *The Cambridge Companion to Herman Melville*. Cambridge, UK: Cambridge University Press, 1998.

D.E.S. Maxwell, *Profiles in Literature: Herman Melville*. New York: Routledge & Kegan Paul, 1968.

Jean-Jacques Mayoux, *Melville*. New York: Evergreen, 1960.

Hershel Parker, *Herman Melville: A Biography*. Vol. 1, 1819–1851. Balitmore: Johns Hopkins University Press, 1996.

Laurie Robertson-Lorant, *Melville: A Biography*. Amherst: University of Massachusetts Press, 1998.

CRITICAL WORKS ON *MOBY-DICK*

Martin Bickman, ed., *Approaches to Teaching Melville's* Moby Dick. New York: Modern Language Association of America, 1985.

Richard H. Brodhead, ed., *New Essays on* Moby-Dick. New York: Cambridge University Press, 1988.

Michael T. Gilmore, ed., *Twentieth Century Interpretations of* Moby-Dick: *A Collection of Critical Essays.* Englewood Cliffs, NJ: Prentice-Hall, 1977.

Kevin J. Hayes, ed., *The Critical Response to Herman Melville's* Moby-Dick. Wesport, CT: Greenwood Press, 1994.

T. Walter Herbert Jr., Moby-Dick *and Calvinism.* New Brunswick, NJ: Rutgers University Press, 1977.

Tyrus Hillway and Luther S. Mansfield, eds., Moby-Dick *Centennial Essays.* Dallas: Southern Methodist University Press, 1953.

Hershel Parker and Harrison Hayford, eds., Moby-Dick *as Doubloon.* New York: W.W. Norton, 1970.

M.O. Percival, *A Reading of* Moby-Dick. New York: Octagon Books, 1967.

Nick Selby, ed., *Herman Melville:* Moby-Dick. New York: Columbia University Press, 1999.

Milton R. Stern, ed., *Discussions of* Moby-Dick. Boston: D.C. Heath, 1960.

VERSIONS OF *MOBY-DICK*

Harrison Hayford and Hershel Parker, eds., *Norton Critical Edition of* Moby-Dick. New York: W.W. Norton, 2001.

Herman Melville, *Moby-Dick* (Enriched Classics Series). New York: Washington Square Press, 1999.

Charles Child Walcott, ed., *Moby-Dick.* New York: Bantam, 1981.

INDEX